Praise for Deepak Chopra

'I absolutely agree with Dr. Chopra's view that "if we want to change the world, we have to begin by changing ourselves." This is the same message that I have always been conveying.'   – The Dalai Lama

'Undoubtedly one of the most lucid and inspired philosophers of our time.'   – Mikhail Gorbachev

'Deepak continues to lead us even deeper into the mysteries and joys of true spirituality.'
– James Redfield, author of
The Celestine Prophecy and *The Secret of Shambhala*

'Deepak Chopra has introduced literally millions of people to the spiritual path, and for this we should all be profoundly grateful.'   – Ken Wilber,
author of *Integral Psychology*

'We have in our midst a spiritual genius.'
– Marianne Williamson,
author of *Return to Love* and *Enchanted Love*

'The rock star of the new spirituality.'   – *Guardian*

'The poet-prophet of alternative medicine.'   – *Time*

'In a coup of conventional wisdom, alternative insight and mind/body medicine, Ch[...] yet another bible for his eager discip[...]

DEEPAK
CHOPRA

Raid on the Inarticulate

The Path to Love

The Seven Spiritual Laws for Parents

The Love Poems of Rumi
(edited by Deepak Chopra; translated
by Deepak Chopra and Fereydoun Kia)

Healing the Heart

Everyday Immortality

The Lords of the Light

On the Shores of Eternity

How to Know God

The Soul in Love

The Chopra Center Herbal Handbook
(with coauthor David Simon)

Grow Younger, Live Longer
(with coauthor David Simon)

The Deeper Wound

The Chopra Center Cookbook
(coauthored by David Simon and
Leanne Backer)

The Angel Is Near

The Daughters of Joy

Golf for Enlightenment

Soulmate

Synchro Destiny

HARNESSING THE INFINITE POWER OF
COINCIDENCE TO CREATE MIRACLES

RIDER
LONDON • SYDNEY • AUCKLAND • JOHANNESBURG

1 3 5 7 9 10 8 6 4 2

First published in 2003 by Harmony Books,
an imprint of Crown Publishing Group, Random House Inc., USA.
This edition published in 2003 by Rider,
an imprint of Ebury Press, Random House,
20 Vauxhall Bridge Road, London SW1V 2SA
www.randomhouse.co.uk

Random House Australia (Pty) Limited
20 Alfred Street, Milsons Point, Sydney,
New South Wales 2061, Australia

Random House South Africa (Pty) Limited
Endulini, 5A Jubilee Road,
Parktown 2193, South Africa

The Random House Group Limited Reg. No. 954009

DESIGN BY ELINA D. NUDELMAN

Papers used by Rider are natural, recyclable products made from
wood grown in sustainable forests.

Printed and bound by Clays Ltd, St Ives Plc

A CIP catalogue record for this book
is available from the British Library

ISBN 1844132218

To Rita, Mallika, Gotham,
Candice, Sumanth, and Tara:

you orchestrate the synchronistic
dance of my universe

CONTENTS

ACKNOWLEDGMENTS

To all the students who have attended Synchrodestiny courses at the Chopra Center over the years; you have validated through experience the knowledge contained in this book;

To Sarah Kelly, Kristin Hutchens, and Jill Romnes, for your vital assistance with those courses;

To my partner, David Simon, for his stimulating and challenging discussions, which continually extend the intellectual horizon;

To Carolyn Rangel, Felicia Rangel, and Anne Marie Girard, for their dedication to this knowledge, and to its advancement;

To my editor, Peter Guzzardi, for his impeccable editing skills, and for his help in preparing this manuscript;

To the staff at the Chopra Center, for your support that makes possible anything I might achieve.

I, the fiery light of divine wisdom,

I ignite the beauty of the plains,

I sparkle the waters.

I burn the sun and the moon and the stars,

With wisdom I order all rightly.

I adorn the earth.

I am the breeze that nurtures all things green.

I am the rain coming from the dew

That causes the grasses to laugh

With the joy of life.

I call forth tears, the aroma of holy work.

I am the yearning for good.

—HILDEGARD OF BINGEN
(1098–1179)

Synchro Destiny

INTRODUCTION

Miracles happen every day. Not just in remote country villages or at holy sites halfway across the globe, but here, in our own lives. They bubble up from their hidden source, surround us with opportunities, and disappear. They are the shooting stars of everyday life. When we see shooting stars, their rarity makes them seem magical, but in fact, they streak across the sky all the time. We just don't notice them during the day, dazzled as we are by sunlight, and at night they emerge only if we happen to look up at the right place in a clear, dark sky.

Although we think of them as extraordinary, miracles also streak across our consciousness every day. We can choose to notice or ignore them, unaware that our destinies may hang in the balance. Tune in to the presence of miracles, and in an instant, life can be transformed into a dazzling experience, more wondrous and exciting than we could even imagine. Ignore it, and an opportunity is gone forever. The question is, Would you recognize a miracle if you saw one? If you recognized it, what would you do? And if you could somehow orchestrate your own miracles, which miracles would you choose?

Beyond your physical self, beyond your thoughts and emotions, there lies a realm within you that is pure potential; from this place anything and everything is possible. Even miracles. Especially miracles. This part of you is interwoven with everything else that exists, and with everything yet to come. I have dedicated my life to exploring and teaching ways to tap into this infinite field of possibilities so that we can redirect and improve our lives materially, emotionally, physically, and spiritually. In previous books I focused on specific outcomes. For example, I've written extensively about attaining perfect health, finding the path to love, and discovering how to know God. This book was written with a broader goal—to guide you to a way of seeing the profound truth that lies behind the illusion of every-day life, and by doing so to discover your true destiny—and how to shape it. This is the path to fulfillment, and eventually to enlightenment.

For more than a decade I have been fascinated by the idea that coincidence is involved in guiding and shaping our lives. We have all experienced events that might be considered amazing or uncanny. Perhaps you were cleaning out a closet and found a gift from someone you hadn't spoken with in years; then an hour later, out of the blue, that person rings you on the phone. You might have read a newspaper article about an experimental skin cancer treatment, and for no apparent reason you decided to save that particular newspaper. A month later, a relative calls to say that he just received a diagnosis of skin cancer—and that information in the article you saved influences his choices and ends up saving his life. Or perhaps your car breaks down on the side of a deserted road, and just when you had resigned yourself to being stranded for hours, the very first vehicle that comes along is a tow truck.

Can such moments be ascribed to mere coincidence? Of course they can, but on closer examination they can also prove to be glimpses of the miraculous. Each time we have an experience like these, we can choose to dismiss it as a random occurrence in a chaotic world, or we can recognize it for the potentially life-altering event it may prove to be. I do not believe in meaningless coincidences. I believe every coincidence is a message, a clue about a particular facet of our lives that requires our attention.

Have you ever listened to that calm, quiet "little voice" deep inside you? Did you ever get a "gut feeling" about something or someone? That little voice and that gut feeling are forms of communication that usually turn out to be well worth heeding. Coincidences are also a kind of message. By paying attention to life's coincidences, you can learn to hear their messages more clearly. And by understanding the forces that shape coincidences, you can come to influence those forces and create your own set of meaningful coincidences, take advantage of the opportunities they present, and experience life as a constantly unfolding miracle that inspires awe in every moment.

Most of us go through life a little afraid, a little nervous, a little excited. We are like children playing hide and seek, wanting to be found, yet hoping we won't be, biting our nails with anticipation. We worry when opportunity approaches a little too closely, and hide deeper in the shadows when fear overcomes us. This is no way to go through life. People who understand the true nature of reality, those whom some traditions call enlightened, lose all sense of fear or concern. All worry disappears. Once you understand the way life really works—the flow of energy, information, and intelligence that directs every moment—then you begin to see the amazing potential in that moment. Mundane things just don't bother you anymore. You become lighthearted and full of joy. You also begin to encounter more and more coincidences in your life.

When you live your life with an appreciation of coincidences and their meanings, you connect with the underlying field of infinite possibilities. This is when the magic begins. This is a state I call *synchrodestiny*, in which it becomes possible to achieve the spontaneous fulfillment of our every desire. Synchrodestiny requires gaining access to a place deep within yourself, while at the same time awakening to the intricate dance of coincidences out in the physical world. It requires understanding the profound nature of things, recognizing the wellspring of intelligence that endlessly creates our universe, and yet having the intention to pursue specific opportunities for change as they appear.

*B*efore we explore this theme in greater depth, let's try a small experiment. Close your eyes and think about what you've been doing over the past twenty-four hours. Then move backward through your memory from where you are right now to where you were exactly one day ago. In your mind's eye, conjure up as much detail as you can about the things you did, the thoughts that passed through your mind, and the feelings that affected your heart.

As you do this, pick one theme or subject from the past twenty-four hours and focus on that particular thought. It doesn't have to be anything especially important or spectacular—just something that you remember dealing with during the day. If you went to the bank, you might choose money or finances. If you had a doctor's appointment, you could choose health. If you played golf or tennis, you could focus on athletics. Consider this theme for a few seconds.

Now, think back five years. Concentrate on today's date, and then work back, year by year, until you reach the same date five years ago. See if you can recall more or less where you were and what you were doing at that time. Try to picture your life at that moment as clearly as you can.

Once you've created a clear mental image of your life as it was five years ago, introduce the theme or subject that you chose to focus on from the past twenty-four hours—finances, health, religion, whatever it was. Now, track your involvement with that subject over the past five years and right up to the present. Try to remember as many incidents as you can in that particular area of your life. If you've chosen health as your topic, for example, you might remember any illnesses you've had, how they might have led you from one doctor to another, how you may have decided to stop smoking and how that may have affected various areas of your life, or the diet you chose, or any of a thousand other possibilities. Go ahead and begin this exercise now.

As you were thinking about your chosen subject, how it evolved in your life and how it affects the way you live now, I'm certain you discovered many "coincidences." So much of life depends on chance meetings, twists of fate, or pathways that suddenly branch out in a new direction. And it is likely that your one topic very quickly connected with many other areas of your life, even if the subject seemed totally insignificant at first. By tracing your personal history in this way you can gain enormous insight into the role that coincidence has played in your life. You can see how, if even one tiny detail had turned out differently, you might have ended up somewhere else, with different people, engaged in different work, moving on an entirely different life trajectory.

Even when you think you have your life all mapped out, things happen that shape your destiny in ways you might never even have imagined. The coincidences or little miracles that happen every day of your life are hints that the universe has much bigger plans for you than you ever dreamed of for yourself. My life, which to others seems to be so well defined, is a perpetual surprise to me. And my past, too, is filled with remarkable coincidences that led me to become who I am today.

My father served in the Indian army as personal physician of Lord Mountbatten, the last

Governor-General of the British Empire in India. While performing his duties my father spent a great deal of time with Lady Mountbatten, and they became friends. Through this friendship my father was encouraged to apply for a scholarship to become a Fellow of the Royal College of Physicians, which took him away to England when I was about six years old. Soon after, my mother also left India to join my father for a while, and my younger brother and I were left in the care of our grandparents.

One day, my father sent a telegram from England saying that he had finally passed all his examinations. This was a momentous day for everyone. My grandfather, so proud of his accomplished son, took us out to celebrate. There had never been such an exciting day as this in our young lives! He took us to the movies, and a carnival, and a family restaurant. He bought us toys and sweets. The whole day was a glorious whirlwind of happiness. But later that night, my brother and I were awakened by the sound of wailing. Although we did not learn this immediately, my grandfather had died, and the sound that had woken us was the anguished cry of women in mourning. His body was taken away and cremated, and his ashes were scattered over the Ganges.

This affected my brother and me profoundly. I lay awake nights wondering where my grandfather was, and whether his soul had survived in some way after his death. My brother had a different reaction—his skin started peeling, as though from a bad sunburn. There was no physical reason for this, so we consulted several doctors. One wise physician recognized that the recent traumatic events in our lives may have left my brother feeling vulnerable and exposed, and that peeling skin was an outward sign of his vulnerability. He predicted that the peeling would stop when my parents returned to India. And, indeed, when they returned, it disappeared.

Looking back I can see that these early events were the seeds of my life's work—my search to understand the nature of the soul, and my studies of the mind-body connection in health. My chosen profession was one long series of coincidences that begins anywhere I choose to look, in this case with my father befriending Lady Mountbatten.

Other seemingly random events influenced me further. When I was in school, my best friend was a young fellow called Oppo. He was very skillful with words. In English class, whenever we had to write an essay, he always got the highest marks. He was also great fun to spend time with. Whatever Oppo did, I wanted to do, too. When Oppo decided he wanted to pursue writing as a career, I made the same choice.

My father's dream for me, however, was that I should become a physician. When we sat down to discuss it I told him, "No. I don't want to be a doctor. I have no interest in medicine. I want to be a great writer one day. I want to write books." Not long after, on my fourteenth birthday, my father gave me some great literature to read, including *Of Human Bondage* by W. Somerset Maugham, *Arrowsmith* by Sinclair Lewis, and *Magnificent Obsession* by Lloyd C. Douglas. Although he didn't mention it at the time, all these books are about doctors. And they made such a deep impression that they sparked in me a desire to become one myself.

Becoming a physician seemed to me to be an ideal way to begin to explore spirituality. I thought that by unraveling the mysteries of the human body, perhaps I could someday get down to the level of the soul. If I had not met Oppo, I might never have developed my love of literature and writing. And if my father had acted differently, fighting me about my decision to be a writer instead of encouraging me with literature about physicians, I might have become a journalist. But these seemingly unrelated events and this web of relationships—from Lady Mountbatten, to my father, to my grandfather and my brother, to Oppo—were synchronized with one another. It was as though a conspiracy of coincidences shaped my personal history and led me to the life I enjoy so thoroughly today.

Each of us is immersed in a network of coincidences that inspire us and help direct our lives. At this very moment, my destiny has led me to write this book, to commune with you through the words on this page. Just the fact that you are reading these words now—that you walked into the library or bookshop, found this book, chose to open the cover, and are investing time and energy to learn about synchrodestiny—is one of those potentially life-altering coincidences. What circumstances brought you to this book? How did you choose this book over the thousands of others? What changes did you think you might like to make in your life as you read through the opening paragraphs?

Seeing the web of coincidence in our lives, however, is just the first stage in understanding and living synchrodestiny. The next stage is to develop an awareness of coincidences while they are happening. It is easy to see them in hindsight, but if you catch coincidences at the moment they occur, you are better positioned to take advantage of the opportunities they may be presenting. Also, awareness translates into energy. The more attention you give to coincidences, the more likely they are to appear, which means you begin to gain greater and greater access to the messages being sent to you about the path and direction of your life.

The final stage of living synchrodestiny occurs when you become fully aware of the interrelatedness of all things, how each affects the next, how they all are "in sync" with one another. "In sync" is a colloquial way of saying "in synchrony," which means operating in unison, as one. Picture a school of fish swimming in one direction, and then in a flash, all the fish change direction. There is no leader giving directions. The fish don't think, "The fish in front of me turned left, so I should turn left." It all happens simultaneously. This synchrony is choreographed by a great, pervasive intelligence that lies at the heart of nature, and is manifest in each of us through what we call the soul.

When we learn to live from the level of the soul, many things happen. We become aware of the exquisite patterns and synchronous rhythms that govern all life. We understand the lifetimes of memory and experience that have molded us into the people we are today. Fearfulness and anxiety fall away as we stand in wonder observing the world as it unfolds. We notice the web of coincidence that surrounds us, and we realize that there is meaning in even the smallest events. We discover that by applying attention and intention to these coincidences, we can create specific outcomes in our lives. We connect with everyone and everything in the universe, and recognize the spirit that unites us all. We unveil the wondrousness that is hidden deep inside us and revel in our newfound glory. We consciously shape our destinies into the limitlessly creative expressions they were meant to be, and by doing so we live out our

most profound dreams, moving closer to enlightenment.

This is the miracle of synchrodestiny.

The pages ahead are divided in two sections.
The first explores the working dynamics of coincidence, synchronicity, and synchrodestiny; it
answers the question "How does this work?" The
second section covers the seven principles of
synchrodestiny, along with day-by-day plans for
using what you learn; it answers the question
"What does this mean for me?"

Those of you who are strongly goal oriented or
have read all my past books may be tempted to
skip right to the lessons, but there are nuances to
the discussion here, along with additional information and focused observations, that you'll want
to understand before proceeding. Also, please
note that over the past ten years the concept of
synchrodestiny has evolved, and it continues to
do so. You may have attended a synchrodestiny
course or listened to tapes in the past, but regard
this volume as both *Synchrodestiny I*, an introduc-
tion to the subject, and *Synchrodestiny II*, a more
advanced and clearer understanding of this phenomenon, both as a theory and as an experience.

For those of you reading this fresh, with no past
experience of my work, I encourage you not to
lose momentum. I have tried hard to make this

book my most accessible to date, and I hope I have succeeded. However, we do grapple with some profound questions, and at times you may feel as though you'll never "get it" all. You will. Try not to get stuck in any one paragraph, or page. Each chapter builds upon the last, and readers usually find that later chapters clarify points that may have been less obvious at first encounter. We have two goals here; one is to understand how synchrodestiny works; the other is to learn specific techniques for harnessing its power to our everyday lives.

This book will not change your life overnight, but if you are willing to devote a little time every day, you will find that miracles are not only possible, they are abundant. Miracles can happen every day, every hour, every minute of your life. At this moment, the seeds of a perfect destiny lie dormant within you. Release their potential and live a life more wondrous than any dream. Let me show you how.

part one

the

PROMISE

of UNLIMITED

POTENTIAL

Matter, Mind, and Spirit

From the moment we become aware of the world around us, we begin to wonder about our place within it. The questions we ask are timeless: Why am I here? How do I fit into the scheme of things? What is my destiny? As children, we tend to think of the future as a clean sheet of paper upon which we can write our own stories. The possibilities seem endless, and we are energized by the promise of discovery and the sheer pleasure of living immersed in so much potential. But as we grow up, become adults, and are "educated" about our limitations, our view of the future becomes constricted. What once lifted our imaginations now weighs us down with dread and anxiety. What once felt boundless becomes narrow and dark.

There is a way to regain the soaring joy of unlimited potential. All that is required is an understanding of the true nature of reality, a willingness to recognize the interrelatedness and inseparability of all things. Then, aided by specific techniques, you will find the world opening up to you, and the good luck and opportunities that popped up every once in a while will occur more and more frequently. How powerful is synchrodestiny? Imagine for a moment that you find yourself with a flashlight in your hand in a room that is totally dark. You turn on the flashlight and see a beautiful painting hanging on the wall. You might think, "Sure, this is a wonderful work of art, but is this all there is?" Then, all at once, the room becomes illuminated from above. You look around and see that you are in an art museum, with hundreds of paintings on the walls around you, each more beautiful than the last. As these possibilities stand revealed to you, you realize you have a lifetime of art to study and love. You are no longer constrained to view just one painting lit by the weak glow of your flashlight.

This is the promise of synchrodestiny. It turns

on the lights. It gives us the ability to make real decisions instead of blind guesses as we move forward in our lives. It allows us to see meaning in the world, to understand the connectedness or synchronicity of all things, to choose the kind of life we want to live, and to fulfill our spiritual journey. With synchrodestiny, we gain the ability to transform our lives according to our intentions.

The first step to living this way is to understand the nature of the three levels of existence.

Level 1:

THE PHYSICAL DOMAIN

The first level of existence is physical or material, the visible universe. This is the world we know best, what we call the real world. It contains matter and objects with firm boundaries, everything that is three-dimensional, and it includes everything we experience with our five senses—all that we can see, hear, feel, taste, or smell. It includes our bodies, the wind, the earth, water, gases, animals, microbes, molecules, and the pages of this book. In the physical domain time seems to flow in a line so straight that we call it the arrow of time, from the past to the present to the future. This means that everything in the physical domain has a beginning, a middle, and an end, and is therefore impermanent. Sentient beings are born and die. Mountains soar from the molten core of the earth and are brought low again by the relentless scouring of rain and wind.

The physical world as we experience it is governed by immutable laws of cause and effect, so that everything is predictable. Newtonian physics allows us to predict action and reaction, so that when billiard balls hit each other with a particular speed and at a particular angle, we can anticipate exactly what route each will travel across the billiards table. Scientists can calculate precisely when a solar eclipse will occur and how long it will last. All of our "commonsense" understanding of the world comes from what we know of this physical domain.

Level 2:
THE QUANTUM DOMAIN

At the second level of existence everything consists of information and energy. This is called the quantum domain. Everything at this level is insubstantial, meaning that it cannot be touched or perceived by any of the five senses. Your mind, your thoughts, your ego, the part of you that you typically think of as your "self" are all part of the quantum domain. These things have no solidity, and yet you know your self and your thoughts to be real. Although it is easiest to think of the quantum domain in terms of mind, it encompasses much more. In fact, everything in the visible universe is a manifestation of the energy and information of the quantum domain. The material world is a subset of the quantum world.

Another way of stating this is that everything in the physical domain is made up of information and energy. In Einstein's famous equation, $E = MC^2$, we learn that energy (E) equals mass (M) times the speed of light (C) squared. This tells us that matter (mass) and energy are the same thing only in different forms—energy *equals* mass.

One of the first science lessons taught in school is that every solid object is made up of molecules, and molecules are made up of even smaller units called atoms. We come to understand that this seemingly solid chair we are sitting on is made up of atoms so small that they cannot be seen without the aid of a powerful microscope. Later in the lesson we learn that tiny atoms are made up of subatomic particles, which have no solidity at all. They are, quite literally, packets or waves of information and energy. This means that, at this second level of existence, the chair you are sitting in is nothing but energy and information.

This concept can be difficult to grasp at first. How can invisible waves of energy and information be experienced as a solid object? The answer is that events in the quantum domain occur at the speed of light, and at that speed our senses simply cannot process everything that contributes to our perceptual experience. We perceive objects as being different from one to the next because energy waves contain different kinds of information, which are determined by the frequency or vibration of those energy waves. It's like listening to the radio. A radio tuned to one station, say 101.5 FM, might play only classical music. Change to a slightly different frequency of radio waves by tuning in to, say, 101.9 FM, and you might hear only rock and roll. Energy is coded for different information depending on how it vibrates.

So the physical world, the world of objects and matter, is made up of nothing but information contained in energy vibrating at different frequencies. The reason we don't see the world as a huge web of energy is that it is vibrating far too fast. Our senses, because they function so slowly, are able to register only chunks of this energy and activity, and these clusters of information become "the chair," "my body," "water," and every other physical object in the visible universe.

This is similar to what happens when we watch a movie. As you know, a motion picture is made up of individual photographic frames with gaps in between frames. If you looked at a movie film on the reel in a projection room, you would see the individual frames and gaps. But when we watch the movie itself, the frames are strung together and played back so fast that our senses no longer observe the frames as discontinuous. Instead, we perceive a steady stream of information.

At the quantum level, the various chunks of energy fields vibrating at different frequencies that we perceive as solid objects are all part of a collective energy field. If we were capable of perceiving everything that was happening at the quantum level, we would see that we are all part of a great "energy soup," and everything—each one of us and all the objects in the physical domain—is just a cluster of energy floating in this energy soup. At any given moment your energy field will come into contact with and affect everyone else's energy field, and each of us responds in some way to that experience. We are all expressions of this communal energy and information. Sometimes we can actually feel this connectedness. This sensation is usually very subtle, but on occasion it becomes more tangible. Most of us have had the experience of walking into a room and sensing "tension so thick you could cut it with a knife," or of being in a church or holy shrine and being engulfed by a sense of peace. That is the collective energy of the environment mingling with your own energy, which you register on some level.

In the physical domain we are also constantly exchanging energy and information. Imagine that you are standing on the street and you smell cigarette smoke from someone walking a block away. This means you are inhaling the breath of that person about one hundred yards away. The smell is just a tracer notifying you that you are inhaling someone else's breath. If the tracer wasn't there, if the person walking by wasn't smoking, you would still be inhaling that person's breath; you just wouldn't know it without cigarette smoke to alert you. And what is breath? It is the carbon dioxide and oxygen that come from the metabolism of every cell in that stranger's body. That is what you are inhaling, just as other people are inhaling your breath. So we are all constantly exchanging bits of ourselves—physical, measurable molecules from our bodies.

At a deeper level, there is really no boundary between our selves and everything else in the world. When you touch an object, it feels solid, as though there was a distinct boundary between it and you. Physicists would say that we experience that boundary as solid because everything is made up of atoms, and the solidity is the sense of atoms bumping against atoms. But consider what an atom is. An atom has a little nucleus with a large cloud of electrons around it. There is no rigid outer shell, just an electron cloud. To visualize this, imagine a peanut in the middle of a football stadium. The peanut represents the nucleus, and the stadium represents the size of the electron cloud around the nucleus. When we touch an object, we perceive solidity when the clouds of electrons meet. That is our interpretation of solidity, given the sensitivity (or relative insensitivity) of our senses. Our eyes are programmed to see objects as three-dimensional and solid. Our nerve endings are programmed to feel objects as three-dimensional and solid. In the reality of the quantum domain, however, there is no solidity. Is there solidity when two clouds meet? No. They meld and separate. Something similar happens whenever you touch another object. Your energy fields (and electron clouds) meet, small portions meld, and then you separate. Although you perceive yourself to be whole, you have lost a bit of your energy field to the object, and have gained a bit of its energy field in return. With every encounter, we exchange information and energy, and we come away changed just a little bit. In this way, too, we can see how connected we are to everything else in the physical world. We are all constantly sharing portions of our energy fields, so all of us, at this quantum level, at the level of our minds and our "selves," are all connected. We are all correlated with one another.

So it is only in our consciousness that our limited senses create a solid world out of pure energy and information. But what if we could see into the quantum domain—if we had "quantum eyes"? In the quantum domain, we would see that everything we think of as solid in the physical world is actually flickering in and out of an infinite void at the speed of light. Just like the frame-and-gap sequence of a motion picture, the universe is an on-off phenomenon. The continuity and solidity of the world exists only in the imagination, fed by senses that cannot discern the waves of energy and information that make up the quantum level of existence. In reality, we are all flickering in and out of existence all the time. If we could fine-tune our senses, we could actually see the gaps in our existence. We are here, and then not here, and then here again. The sense of continuity is held only by our memories.

There is an analogy that illustrates this point. Scientists know that it takes a snail about three seconds to register light. So imagine that a snail was watching me, and that I left the room, robbed a bank, and came back in three seconds. As far as the snail was concerned, I never left the room. I could take her to court and she would provide a perfect alibi. For the snail, the time that I was gone from the room would fall into one of those gaps between the frames of flickering existence. Her sense of continuity, assuming snails have one, would simply not register the gap.

So the sensory experience of all living beings is a purely artificial perceptual construct created in the imagination. There is a Zen story in which two monks are looking at a flag that is waving in the wind. The first one says, "The flag is waving." The second one says, "No, the wind is moving." Their teacher comes over and they pose him the question. "Who's right? I say the flag is moving. He says the wind is moving." The teacher says, "You are both wrong. Only consciousness is moving." As consciousness moves, it imagines the world into existence.

So the mind is a field of energy and information. Every idea is also energy and information. You have imagined your physical body and the whole physical world into existence by perceiving energy soup as distinct physical entities. But where does the mind responsible for this imagination come from?

Level 3:

THE NONLOCAL DOMAIN

The third level of existence consists of intelligence, or consciousness. This can be called the virtual domain, the spiritual domain, the field of potential, the universal being, or nonlocal intelligence. This is where information and energy emerge from a sea of possibilities. The most fundamental, basic level of nature is not material; it is not even energy and information soup; it is pure potential. This level of nonlocal reality operates beyond the reach of space and time, which simply do not exist at this level. We call it nonlocal because it cannot be confined by a location—it is not "in" you or "out there." It simply is.

The intelligence of the spiritual domain is what organizes "energy soup" into knowable entities. It is what binds quantum particles into atoms, atoms into molecules, molecules into structures. It is the organizing force behind all things. This can be a slippery concept to grasp. One relatively simple way of thinking about this virtual domain is to recognize the dual nature of your own thoughts. As you read these words, your eyes are seeing the black print on the page, and your mind is translating the print into symbols—letters and words—and then trying to deduce their meaning. But take a step back and ask, Who is it that is doing the reading? What is the consciousness that underlies your thoughts? Become aware of the duality of these interior processes. Your mind is busy decoding, analyzing, and translating. So who is doing the reading? With this one little twist of attention you may become aware that there is a presence within you, a force that is always doing the experiencing. This is the soul, or nonlocal intelligence, and its experience takes place at the virtual level.

Just as information and energy forge the physical world, this nonlocal domain ("without location") creates and orchestrates the activity of information and energy. According to best-selling author and metaphysical pioneer Larry Dossey, M.D., nonlocal events have three important qualities that distinguish them from events confined to the physical world: They are correlated, and this correlation is *unmediated*, *unmitigated*, and *immediate*. Let's briefly explore what he means by this.

The behavior of two or more subatomic events is *acausally interrelated*, meaning that "one event is not the cause of another event, yet the behavior of one is immediately correlated or coordinated with the other." In other words, they seem to be dancing to the same tune, even though they are not communicating with each other in the conventional sense. This is the meaning of *unmediated*.

The correlation between these nonlocal events is also *unmitigated*, which means that the strength of the correlation remains undiminished with distance in space and time. For example, if you and I were in a room talking, my voice would sound very different than if we were standing across the street from each other. At that greater distance my voice would sound much weaker, if you could hear me at all. If you were in the nonlocal domain, I would be heard clearly, *regardless of whether I was standing right next to you, across the street, a mile away, or even on another continent.*

Third, *immediate* means that no travel time is needed for nonlocal events. We are all familiar with the fact that light and sound travel at different speeds, which is why we see lightning in the distance before we hear the rumble of thunder. With nonlocal events there is no such lag time, because nonlocal correlations do not follow the laws of classical physics. There is no signal, there is no light, and there is no sound. There is no "thing" that has to travel. Correlations between events that occur at the nonlocal or virtual level occur instantly, without cause, and without any weakening over time or distance.

Nonlocal intelligence is everywhere at once, and can cause multiple effects simultaneously in various locations. It is from this virtual domain that everything in the world is organized and synchronized. This, then, is the source of the coincidences that are so important to synchrodestiny. When you learn to live from this level, you can spontaneously fulfill your every desire. You can create miracles.

EVIDENCE FOR THE
VIRTUAL DOMAIN

The virtual domain is not a figment of the imagination, the result of some human longing for a universal force greater than ourselves. Although philosophers have been discussing and debating the existence of "spirit" for thousands of years, it wasn't until the twentieth century that science could offer proof of the existence of nonlocal intelligence. Although the following discussion is somewhat involved, if you read it through to the end, I hope you will be filled with the same sense of wonder and excitement that I felt when I first learned of this work.

As most of us learned in science class, the universe is made up of both solid particles and waves. We were taught that particles were the building blocks of all the solid objects in the world. For example, we learned that the very smallest units of matter, such as the electrons in an atom, were particles. Similarly, we were taught that waves—such as sound and light waves—were nonsolid. There was never confusion between the two; particles were particles, and waves were waves.

Physicists then discovered that a subatomic particle is part of what is known as a wave packet. Although waves of energy are typically continuous, with equally spaced peaks and troughs, a wave packet is a concentration of energy. (Imagine a little ball of static, with quick, sharp peaks and troughs representing the amplitude of the wave.)

Wave

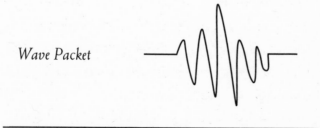

Wave Packet

There are two questions we might ask about the particle in this wave packet: (1) Where is it, and (2) what is its momentum? Physicists discovered that you can ask one of these questions, but not both. For example, once you ask "Where is it?" and you fix a wave-particle in a location, it becomes a particle. If you ask "What is its momentum?" you have decided that movement is the critical factor; therefore you must be talking about a wave.

So is this thing we are talking about, the "wave-particle," a particle or a wave? It depends on which of the two questions we decide to ask. At any given moment, that wave-particle can be *either* a particle *or* a wave because we can't know both the location and the momentum of the wave-particle. In fact, as it turns out, until we measure either its location or its momentum, it is *both particle and wave simultaneously*. This concept is known as the Heisenberg Uncertainty Principle, and it is one of the fundamental building blocks of modern physics.

Imagine a closed box with a wave-particle in it. Its absolute identity is not fixed until it is observed or measured in some way. At the moment before observation, its identity is pure potential. It is both wave and particle, and it exists only in the virtual domain. After observation or measurement takes place, the potential "collapses" into a single entity—either particle or wave. Given our usual, sense-based way of evaluating the world, the idea that a thing can exist in more than one state at the same time is totally counterintuitive. But this is the wonder of the quantum world.

A famous thought experiment by physicist

Erwin Schrödinger points out the kinds of odd occurrences that are made possible by quantum physics. Imagine that you have a closed box that contains a wave-particle, a cat, a lever, and a bowl of cat food with a loose lid. If the wave-particle becomes a particle, it will trip the lever, which will flip the lid off the bowl of food, and the cat will eat. If the wave-particle becomes a wave, the lid stays on the food. If we open the box (thereby making an observation), we will see either an empty bowl of cat food (and a happy cat) or a full bowl (and a hungry cat). It all depends on the type of observation we make. Now here's the part that boggles the mind: Before we look in the box and make an observation, the bowl is *both* empty and full, and the cat is *simultaneously* fed and hungry. At that moment, both possibilities exist at the same time. *It is the observation alone that turns possibility into reality.* As remarkable as this might seem, physicists recently completed an experiment proving this phenomenon by demonstrating that a charged, unobserved beryllium atom was capable of being in two separate locations at the same time!

*P*erhaps even more mind-boggling is the notion that the very idea of two separate locations may be a perceptual artifact. In other words, two correlated events in two different locations might in fact be the movements of a single event. Imagine a single fish in a tank, with two video cameras recording its movements. The two cameras are at right angles to each other and project their respective images to two separate video screens in another room. You are sitting in this room looking at both screens. You see two different fish and you are amazed when one fish turns or moves in a certain direction and its behavior is immediately correlated with the behavior of the other fish. Of course you do not know what is happening behind the scenes. If you did, you would see that there is only one fish! If we placed many different cameras at many different angles, and projected these images to different screens in the same room, you would be amazed that all these different fish are in instant communicational correlation with one another.

Great seers from mystical traditions suggest that what we experience every day is a projected reality where events and things only "appear" to be separate in space and time. In the deeper realm we are all members of the same body, and when one part of the body moves, every single part of that body is instantly affected.

Scientists also propose a level of existence called Minkowski's eight-dimensional hyperspace. In this mathematically conceived dimension the distance between two events, no matter how separate they appear to be in space-time, is always zero. This once again suggests a dimension of existence where we are all inseparably one. Separation may just be an illusion. When we feel love in any form, it has the effect of beginning to shatter that illusion.

Because observation is the key to defining the wave-particle as a single entity, Niels Bohr and other physicists believed that consciousness alone was responsible for the collapse of the wave-particle. It might be said, then, that without consciousness, everything would exist only as undefined, potential packets of energy, or pure potential.

This is one of the key points of this book. Let me repeat it because it is so important: *Without consciousness acting as an observer and interpreter, everything would exist only as pure potential.* That pure potential is the virtual domain, the third level of existence. It is nonlocal and can't be depleted; it is unending and all-encompassing. Tapping into that potential is what allows us to make miracles.

Miracles is not too strong a word. Let me return to physics to describe how scientists have documented some of the astounding events that can occur from this level of potential.

Intrigued and troubled by the possibilities suggested by quantum physics, Albert Einstein devised his own thought experiment: Imagine creating two identical wave-particles that are then shot off in opposite directions. What happens if we ask about the location of wave-particle A and ask about the momentum of wave-particle B? Remember, the particles are identical, so whatever measurement is calculated for one will, by definition, hold true for the other. Knowing the location of wave-particle A (and thus collapsing it into a particle) simultaneously tells us the location of wave-particle B, and therefore also collapses it into a particle.

The implications of this thought experiment (which has been confirmed mathematically as well as experimentally) are enormous. If observing wave-particle A affects wave-particle B, that means that some nonlocal connection or communication is occurring in which information is exchanged faster than the speed of light, without the exchange of energy. That is contrary to every commonsense view of the world. This thought experiment is known as the Einstein-Podolsky-Rosen paradox. And indeed, laboratory experiments have shown that the laws of quantum physics do hold up, and that nonlocal communication or connection is a reality.

Let me try to illustrate the magnitude of this point with an example that is a bit of an exaggeration, but at least it takes place in the physical world so its effects are easier to see. Imagine that a company simultaneously sends out two identical packages, one to me in California, and one to you at your home. In each of the boxes is a correlated, unobserved wave-particle, pure potential. You and I receive and open our packages at exactly the same moment. Just before I cut the tape and open the flaps, I create a mental picture of what

I want the box to contain. When I open the box, I find that it contains just what I imagined, a violin. But that's only half the miracle. When you open your box, it also contains a violin! When I imagined what I wanted the box to contain, the wave-particles collapsed into a specific form. And whatever I imagined also affected the wave-particles in your package. We could repeat this experiment over and over again, and we'd always have the same outcome: Whatever I imagine for myself is matched, at the exact same moment, for you. Not only can I influence the form of one set of wave-particles, but the wave-particles are somehow able to communicate the form they are taking across the distance from my house to yours, faster than the speed of light. This is what is meant by nonlocal communication or correlation.

*I*nteresting experiments have been performed by researcher Cleve Baxter, an associate and friend of ours at the Chopra Center. In 1972 he developed a methodology for studying human cells that had been isolated from a person's body. For example, in one of his experiments, he took human spermatozoa and studied them in a test tube by electroding them and measuring their electromagnetic activity using EEG-type instrumentation. The sperm donor was located in a room about forty feet down the hall from the lab. When the sperm donor crushed a capsule of amyl nitrate and inhaled the fumes there was an instantaneous spike in the electromagnetic activity of the lab sperm three rooms away.

One day Cleve Baxter was isolating white cells in order to study them, and a very interesting thing happened. As part of the procedure he centrifuged his saliva to get a concentrated number of white cells, then placed them in a small test tube and inserted gold wire electrodes connected to EEG-type instrumentation. He had the sudden idea to inflict a small cut on the back of his hand to see if this might affect his white cells. He went to search for a sterile lancet on a nearby shelf. When he came back he glanced at the chart that was recording the electromagnetic activity of the white blood cells: It had already registered intense activity among the white blood cells during his search for the lancet. In other words, his white cells were reacting to his *intention* to cut his hand even before he actually inflicted the cut.

On another occasion Cleve Baxter was training a colleague of his to collect oral leukocytes. Somehow they got into a discussion about an article in *Playboy* magazine, an interview with William Shockley, a scientist who was very controversial at the time. Cleve Baxter suddenly remembered that his partner had a copy of that particular issue of the magazine in his office desk. He dashed off, found the issue under discussion, and brought it up to the lab. By this time, Steve, his lab associate, had finished the cell collection and had electroded his cells. Cleve Baxter then aimed one video camera, mounted on a tripod, over Steve's shoulder to allow for later correlation of what Steve would be viewing. Another video camera was mounted over the chart recording in progress. The two video camera images were then combined through split-screen technology. This ensured that there would be an accurate record of the timing of possible reactions. As Steve leafed through the *Playboy* magazine to find the article, he came across the centerfold featuring Bo Derek in her nothingness. According to Cleve Baxter, "Even as Steve said aloud 'I don't think she's a ten,' his white cells in the test tube showed a full-scale reaction, hitting the top and bottom limit stops on the chart recorder." After two full minutes of continuous reactivity, Cleve Baxter suggested that Steve close the magazine. When he did so his electroded cells calmed down. Then, a minute later, when Steve reached over to reopen the closed magazine, the cells spiked again. Cleve Baxter states, "When Steve experienced this high-quality observation, knowing the feelings and thoughts of his own mind, it put an end to any skepticism."

Cleve Baxter has performed many similar experiments revealing that the cells of all biological organisms, including plants and a variety of bacteria, have biocommunication ability. All living cells have a cellular consciousness and are able to communicate with other cells of the same or other species even when they are a distance apart. Moreover, this communication is instantaneous. Since distance in space is also distance in time, one could therefore say that events separated from each other in time, occurring either in the past or in the future, could be instantly correlated.

In an extension of this research, nonlocal communication has been demonstrated in people, too. In the famous Grinberg-Zylberbaum experiment, published in 1987, scientists used a device known as an electroencephalograph to measure the brain waves of two people meditating together. They found that some pairs of people they measured showed a strong correlation in their brain wave patterns, suggesting a close bond or mental relationship. These meditators could identify when they felt that they were in "direct communication" with each other, and this was confirmed by the machines measuring their brain waves. These strongly bonded pairs were asked to meditate together, side by side, for twenty minutes. Then one of the meditators was taken to a different room that was closed and isolated. With each person in a separate room, the meditators were asked to try to establish direct communication with each other. The meditator who had been moved was then stimulated by bright lights flashing in the room, which caused little spikes in his brain waves called evoked potentials. Because the brain waves of both meditators were still being measured, the scientists were able to see that the meditator who was exposed to light did, indeed, show the little spikes of evoked potentials. But the fascinating part of this experiment is that *the meditator who was not exposed to the light also showed little spikes of brain waves* that corresponded to the evoked potentials of the light-exposed meditator. So these two people were connected at a deep level (via meditation), and that connection allowed for measurable physical reactions even in the person who was not exposed to the light stimulation. What happened to one person also happened to the other, automatically and instantly.

These results cannot be explained by any means except nonlocal correlation, which occurs in the virtual domain, the level of the spirit that connects, orchestrates, and synchronizes everything. This boundless field of intelligence or consciousness is everywhere, manifesting itself in everything. We've seen it operate at the level of the subatomic particle—the building block of all things—and we've seen it connect two people at a level that transcends separation. But you need not go into a laboratory to see this nonlocal intelligence at work. Proof is all around us, in animals, in nature, and even in our own bodies.

Synchronicity in Nature

2

We see examples of synchronicity in nature so often that they begin to seem ordinary. But look again with eyes that are tuned in to the near-impossibility of what's taking place, and the concept of synchronicity will begin to make sense. For example, look up at the sky on any summer's day and wait for a flock of birds. Like the school of fish I mentioned earlier, they all seem to be moving in formation; when they change direction, they all execute the same motions synchronistically.

A single flock of birds can include hundreds of individuals, yet each bird moves in harmony with every other bird without an obvious leader. They change direction in an instant, all birds altering their course at the exact same moment, and they do it perfectly. You never see birds bumping into each other in flight. They climb and turn and swoop so that they look like a single organism, as if some unspoken command was issued that they all obeyed at once. How is that happening? There's not enough time for any exchange of information, so any correlation of activity among the birds must be happening nonlocally.

Physicists have been working for years to discover the properties that guide the movements of birds, and so far they have been unsuccessful. The complexity and absolute precision of the birds' behavior stumps physical science every time. Engineers have been studying the movements of birds to see if there is a way to discover principles that might translate into solutions for traffic jams. If they could somehow harness the sensory mechanism used by birds and translate it into guidelines for road or car design, then there might never be another car accident. We would know in advance what every other car on the road was going to do at every moment. This project will never succeed, however, because there is no analogy that can be brought to the mechanical world. The instantaneous communication we commonly see in flocks of birds and schools of fish comes from the spiritual level, the organizing nonlocal intelligence in the virtual domain. The result is synchronicity, beings that are totally in tune with their environment and with each other, dancing to the rhythm of the cosmos.

Although birds and fish provide the most striking example of synchronicity in nature, there are as many examples as there are creatures on earth. All social creatures show evidence of nonlocal communication, and extensive studies have been conducted with insects and herd animals showing that their responses to threats are immediate, quicker than could be explained by normal communication methods.

Scientist Rupert Sheldrake has conducted some fascinating studies of what seem to be cases of nonlocal communication between dogs and their human companions. People and dogs can form very close bonds, and Sheldrake has documented cases in which dogs seem to know when their owners are coming home. From ten minutes to two hours before the owner arrives, the dog will sit at the front door and wait, as if anticipating the owner's return. Skeptics have said that this was simply a case of habit, that the owner comes home at a specific time each day, or that the dog can hear the car or smell the owner from miles away. But these dogs are able to predict their owners' arrival even when he or she comes home at unexpected times, or by a different car, or on foot, or even if the wind is blowing in the opposite direction, so that there is no possible way the owner's scent could reach the house.

This doesn't happen with all dogs or all owners, but when it does, it is a very powerful phenomenon. Even more startling, Sheldrake has demonstrated that dogs can pick up on intention. Let's say the owner is in Paris on a two-week vacation, and the dog is at home in London. If the owner suddenly changes plans and decides to go home a week early, the dog shows the same signs of anticipation a week early. As soon as the owner thinks, "It's time to go home," the dog gets up from wherever he has been sleeping and sits at the front door wagging his tail, waiting for the owner's arrival.

To make sure that these observations weren't just a matter of wishful thinking on the owners' part, studies looked at how specific dogs reacted to their owners' intentions to come home. Video cameras were set up in the house and focused on places the dog was likely to be—his bed, the front door, the kitchen. The owner would go out with no idea of where she was going or when she would return home; that determination was made by the scientists. Only after she got into her car was she given instructions about where to go. Later, at random times, a scientist would page the dog's owner to signal that it was time to start home. The time was noted and compared to the actions of the dog on the videotapes. As the owner started for home, the dog would almost always go to the door and await her return, regardless of where she was, or what time it was, or how long it would be until she actually arrived home.

There's no doubt that certain people have a very strong connection with their dogs; they are *correlated* with their dogs. They are synchronized. And through this bond the owner and dog experience nonlocal communication.

Examples of synchronicity can be found most often in the animal world because animals are more in touch with the essential nature of things. We humans lose our sense of connectedness in a welter of concerns about rent payments, which car to buy, or any of a million other distractions. As soon as we develop an ego, a sense of "I" that is different from everyone else, those connections are obscured.

But some people do experience strong synchronicity, and they don't need to be meditators. We've all heard stories of identical twins who can readily tune in to what the other twin is feeling or thinking. This same kind of connection can be seen in other strongly bonded individuals. I was talking with a patient once when he suddenly had a piercing pain in his abdomen and began rolling around on the floor. When I asked what happened, he replied, "It feels like somebody stabbed me over here." Later we found out that at that precise moment his mother had been mugged in Philadelphia and stabbed in the abdomen. He had a very strong connection to his mother; it was easily the most important relationship in his life. They were so closely attuned that, at some level, their physiology was as one. We could say that they were *entrained*.

Entrainment is just another word for *correlation* or *synchronization;* it is used most often by scientists to describe the state of being "caught up" by another substance or force. For example, particles can be entrained in a stream of liquid and flow along immersed in it. The word helps us describe how things become correlated with each other. Remember, synchronicity occurs only when people, animals, or objects have some close relationship, or are entrained.

In one example of entrainment, field researchers have observed African tribes in which mothers have very close relationships with their children, starting with their unborn babies. At the moment of conception, the mother will choose a name and then write a song for her baby. She sings this song throughout pregnancy, while the baby is still in the womb. When the baby is being delivered, all the neighbors come and they sing the song for the baby, too. Later, at every important milestone, they'll sing that baby's song: on birthdays, at the initiation when the baby becomes a young child, during puberty rites, at the engagement and wedding. The song becomes the anchor for the original bond between mother and baby, and even extends beyond death, when the song is sung at the person's funeral. This is one way the child is entrained into the world of the mother and the tribe. It creates such an intimate connection that if the baby is somewhere in the bushes and the mother is out in the fields, if the baby feels discomfort of any kind, the mother will experience the same discomfort in her body at that very moment.

Another well-known example of nonlocal communication between mother and child is the leakage of breast milk when the child cries out with hunger, even if the two people are in different locations.

The meditators I described in the previous chapter knew and liked each other before the experiment, but they were further entrained by the meditation itself. It's one thing to be connected socially, to be husband and wife, or sisters or brothers, but for nonlocal communication to occur there must be a deeper connection as well. Put that way, it sounds as though it must be terribly difficult to make this sort of connection. But in fact we are all constantly in touch with nonlocal intelligence. The very fact that our bodies exist at all is totally dependent on nonlocal communication.

How can something as real and substantial as our bodies depend on virtual communication? Consider that the human body consists of approximately one hundred trillion cells, about one thousand cells for every bright star in the Milky Way. It takes only fifty replications, starting with the one-celled fertilized ovum, to produce those one hundred thousand billion cells. The first replication gives you two cells. The second replication gives you four. The third replication gives you sixteen cells, and so on. By the fiftieth replication, you have one hundred thousand billion cells in your body, and that's where the replication stops.

So all of the cells of your body start from just one cell. That one cell replicates and replicates, and somewhere along the line the cells differentiate. There are some 250 different types of cells in the human body, from the spherical simple fat cell to the thin, branching nerve cell. Scientists still have no idea how that one cell ends up dividing into so many different kinds of cells, which then are able to organize themselves into a stomach, a brain, skin, teeth, and all the other highly specialized parts of the body.

In addition to doing its specific job in the body, each cell does a few million things per second just to keep functioning: creating proteins, adjusting the permeability of its membrane, and processing nutrients, to name just a few. Each cell also has to know what every other cell is doing; otherwise your body would fall apart. The human body can function only if it is operating synchronistically, and all this can happen only through nonlocal correlation. How else could one hundred trillion cells each doing one million things per second coordinate their activities so as to support a living, breathing human being? How else could a human body generate thoughts, remove toxins, and smile at a baby, or even make a baby, all at the same time?

In order to wiggle my toes, first I have the thought that I'd like to do so. The thought activates my brain cortex, which then sends a nerve impulse down through the spinal cord into my legs and moves my toes. That in itself is miraculous. Where did the thought come from? Before the thought, there was no energy, but as soon as I had the thought and the intention to wiggle my toes, it created a controlled electromagnetic storm in my brain, which transferred down the nerve, and caused it to discharge a certain chemical. Then my toes wiggled. That's a very linear, mechanical, and local phenomenon—except for that very first part, the thought that started it all. How did the thought first create the electricity? Scientists understand the body's mechanisms—action potential, neurotransmitters, and muscular contractions, all of it. But no one can show through experiment where the thought came from. The thought cannot be seen, but without it, we would be paralyzed. No thought, no toe-wiggling. Somehow your awareness becomes information and energy. Where does that happen?

The answer is that the thought originates in the virtual domain.

Our bodies behave synchronistically all the time. Whenever there's even a slight perturbation in our physical body, the whole body reacts. For example, suppose you haven't eaten all day, so your blood sugar level starts to drop. Immediately, a whole synchronicity of events works to bring your blood sugar back up. The pancreas secretes a hormone called glucagon, which converts stored sugar in the liver into glucose, which immediately becomes available for energy. In addition, fat cells release fatty acids and glucose into the bloodstream, and the nervous system stimulates skeletal muscles to give up their glucose stores. All these things happen at once. Insulin levels will go down and your heart rate will speed up to mobilize energy. Nearly a million things will happen in the body with the intention of bringing that sugar level back to normal. And that is just one function among all the others occurring simultaneously throughout the body. All this could be possible only through nonlocal communication, information correlated faster than the speed of light, outside the bounds of standard physics.

It has been suggested that this nonlocal communication is set up by the resonance of the electrical activity of our hearts. Your heart has something called a pacemaker, which keeps the normal heart beating at about seventy-two times per minute. The pacemaker in your heart sets off an electrical impulse every few seconds, and that electrical impulse causes the mechanical contraction of your heart. Any time you have an electrical current, you have an electromagnetic field around it. (Electromagnetic fields are basically photons behaving in a certain way.) So the heart, with every beat, broadcasts its electromagnetic energy to the rest of your body. It even sends its electromagnetic field outside the body (if the field is amplified, other people can register receiving these signals!). The energy is sent throughout your body. In this way, the heart is the master oscillator of the body, with its own electromagnetic field. It creates a field of resonance so that every cell in the body starts to entrain with every other cell, which makes every cell synchronistically attuned to every other cell.

When cells are caught in the same field of resonance, they are all dancing to the same music. Studies show that when we're thinking creatively, or when we are feeling peaceful, or when we're feeling love, those emotions generate a very coherent electromagnetic field. And that electromagnetic field is broadcast to the rest of your body. It also creates a field of resonance where all the cells of the body lock in with each other. Every cell knows what every other cell is doing because they're all doing the same thing, while still expressing their unique functions efficiently: Stomach cells are making hydrochloric acid, immune cells are generating antibodies, the pancreatic cells are manufacturing insulin, and so on.

In a healthy body, this synchronicity is perfectly regulated. Healthy people are firmly locked into these rhythms. When disease occurs, one of those rhythms has gone awry. Stress is the biggest disrupter. If you're stressed, if you're feeling hostility, your body's balance gets thrown off. Stress breaks our nonlocal connection with everything else. When you are experiencing disease ("disease"), then some part of your body is beginning to get constricted. It is tuning itself out from the nonlocal field of intelligence.

There are many emotions that can cause a disruption of the electromagnetic field in the heart, but the ones that have been most precisely documented are anger and hostility. Once this synchronization is disrupted, your body starts to behave in a fragmented manner. The immune system gets suppressed, which leads to other problems, such as increased susceptibility to cancer, infections, and accelerated aging. This effect is so strong that animals can pick it up. If a dog sees a person who is harboring hostility, it will bark and act ferocious. Wherever you go, you are broadcasting who you are at this very intimate level.

But our connection with nonlocal intelligence doesn't end at the boundary of our bodies. Just as our bodies are in balance, so the universe is in balance also, and it displays that balance in rhythms or cycles.

As it travels around the sun, the earth creates seasonal rhythms. Winter turns to spring, and birds start to migrate, fish seek their spawning grounds, flowers bloom, trees bud, fruit ripens, eggs hatch. That one change in nature—a slight tilt of the earth—initiates a cascade of nonlocal events. All of nature is acting as if it were one organism. Even people feel different during various seasons. Some people tend to get depressed in the winter, and to fall in love in spring. Biochemically, certain changes in your body correspond to the movement of our planet. All of nature is a symphony, and we are part of it.

As the earth spins on its axis, it gives us something called a circadian, or daily, rhythm. Nocturnal creatures awaken at night and go to sleep during the day. Birds forage for food at specific times known as bird hours. Our bodies are also synchronized to circadian rhythms. I spend most of my time in California, and without conscious effort, my body falls into a California rhythm in keeping with my time zone. My body begins to anticipate the sunrise, allowing me to awaken at about the same time every day, and it slows down in evening, allowing me to prepare for sleep. During sleep, my body is still highly active, moving me through the different stages of sleep, changing my brain waves. Hormones that control and regulate different body functions are still being produced and secreted, but in different amounts than during my awakening hours. Each cell still carries on its million different activities, as the body as a whole conducts its nighttime cycle.

On earth, we feel the effects of the sun in the

circadian rhythm, and the effects of the moon in the lunar rhythm, as it waxes and wanes. The cycles of the moon play themselves out in our body, instantly correlating with planetary movements. A woman's twenty-eight-day menstrual cycle is affected by the moon, and there are other, more subtle monthly rhythms that affect mood and productivity in all people. The gravitational effects of the sun and moon on the earth cause ocean tides, which also affect our bodies. After all, millions of years ago we, too, were inhabitants of the ocean. When we slithered onto shore we brought some of the ocean along with us. Eighty percent of our body has the same chemical composition as the ocean we once called home, and is still affected by its tidal pull.

All these rhythms—circadian, lunar, and seasonal—are tuned in to each other. There are rhythms within rhythms within rhythms. And these drumbeats echo all around us and within us. We are not outsiders to the process; we are part of it, throbbing to the pulse of the universe. Nonlocal intelligence is within us and all around us. It is spirit, the potential from which everything emerges. It is the ground of our being; it is dimensionless; it has no volume, no energy, no mass, and it occupies no space. Nor does it exist in time. All experiences are localized projections of this nonlocal reality, which is a singular, unified potential. Here everything is inseparably one. At this deeper level of reality you *are* this nonlocal intelligence, a universal being observing itself through a human nervous system. Just as a prism breaks up a single beam of light into the colors of the spectrum, nonlocal intelligence, by observing itself, breaks a single reality into a multitude of appearances.

Think of the universe as a single, huge organism. Its vastness is a perceptual, projected reality; even though "out there" you may be seeing a big football stadium filled with thousands of people, the real phenomenon is a small electrical impulse inside your brain that you, the nonlocal being, interpret as a football game. Yoga Vasishta, an ancient Vedic text, says, "The world is like a huge city, reflected in a mirror. So too, the universe is a huge reflection of yourself in your own consciousness."

It is, in short, the soul of all things.

The Nature of the Soul

3

In the vastness of the ocean, there is no ego. Seen from a great distance, from the moon or a satellite, the ocean looks calm and inanimate, a large swath of blue girdling the earth. But as we get closer and closer to the ocean itself, we see that it is in constant motion, roiled by currents and tides, eddies and waves. We see these ocean patterns as distinct entities. As each wave is created, we can watch it crest, break, and race to the shore. Yet it is impossible to separate the wave from the ocean. You cannot take a bucket, scoop out a wave, and bring it home. If you take a photo of a wave and come back the next day, no wave will be an exact match.

When we are beginning to understand the soul, the ocean provides a wonderful analogy. Imagine the ocean as nonlocal reality, the field of infinite possibilities, the virtual level of existence that synchronizes everything. Each of us is like a wave in that ocean. We are created from it, and it makes up the very core of who we are. Just as a wave takes on a specific shape, we, too, take on intricate patterns of nonlocal reality. This vast, unending ocean of possibility is the essence of everything in the physical world. The ocean represents the nonlocal, and the wave represents the local. The two are intimately connected.

Once we define the soul as deriving from the nonlocal, or virtual, realm, then our place in the universe becomes remarkably clear: We are both local and nonlocal, an individual pattern emerging from nonlocal intelligence, which is also part of everyone and everything else. We can think of the soul, then, as having two parts. The vast, nonlocal soul exists at the virtual or spirit level. It is powerful, pure, and capable of anything. The personal, local part of the soul exists at the quantum level. This is what reaches into our daily lives and holds the essence of who we are. It, too, is powerful, pure, and capable of anything. The same unbounded potential of the infinite spirit also resides in each and every one of us. Our personal soul, which we think of when we think of our "selves," is an outcropping of the eternal soul.

If we could learn to live from the level of the soul, we would see that the best, most luminous part of ourselves is connected to all the rhythms of the universe. We would truly know ourselves as the miracle-makers we are capable of being. We would lose fear, and longing, and hatred, and anxiety, and hesitation. Living from the level of the soul means diving past the ego, past the limitations of the mind that harness us to events and outcomes in the physical world.

In the vastness of the ocean there is no individual "I" clamoring for attention. There are waves and eddies and tides, but it is all, in the end, ocean. We are all patterns of nonlocality pretending to be people. In the end, it is all spirit.

And yet, we all *feel* quite individual, don't we? Our senses reassure us that these bodies are real, and we think our own very personal, individual thoughts. We learn, fall in love, have children, and work at our own careers. How is it that we do not feel this vast ocean churning inside us? Why do our lives feel so circumscribed? It all comes back to the three levels of existence.

At the physical level, what we call the real world, the soul is the observer in the midst of the observation. Anytime you observe something, there are three components involved. The first, which occurs in the physical world, is the object of your observation. The second, which happens at the level of the mind, is the process of observing. The third component of observation is the actual observer, which we call the soul.

Let's look at a simple example of the three components of observation. First, a four-legged, furry animal becomes the object of your observation. Next, your eyes receive the visual image of the object and transmit the signal to your mind, which interprets that object to be a dog. But *who* is observing the dog? Turn your awareness inward and you become aware of a presence within you. That presence is your soul, the extension of the vast nonlocal intelligence that is cropping up in you. So the mind is involved in the process of knowing, but the soul is the knower. This presence, this awareness, this knower, this soul, is unchanging. It is the still point of reference in the midst of all the changing scenery in the physical world.

We each have a soul, but because we are each observing from a different place and a different set of experiences, we do not observe the same things in exactly the same ways. The variations in what we observe are based on our minds' interpretations. If you and I both were to observe a dog, for instance, we would have different thoughts. I may see it as a ferocious animal, and I may become afraid. You may look at the same dog and see it as a friendly companion. Our minds interpret the observation differently. When I see a dog, I run. When you see a dog, you whistle and play with it.

Interpretation happens at the level of the mind, but it is our individual souls that are conditioned by experience, and through that memory of past experience the soul influences our choices and interpretations in life. These tiny kernels or seeds of memory build up in the individual soul over a lifetime, and this combination of memory and imagination based on experience is called karma. Karma accumulates in the personal part of the soul, the wave at the core of our being, and colors it. This personal soul governs the conscience and provides a template for the kind of person each of us will turn out to be. In addition, the actions we take can affect this personal soul, and change our karma, for better or worse.

The universal, nonlocal part of the soul is not touched by our actions, but is connected to a spirit that is pure and unchanging. In fact, the definition of *enlightenment* is "the recognition that I am an infinite being seeing and seen from, observing and observed from, a particular and localized point of view." Whatever else we are, no matter how much of a mess we may have made of our lives, it is always possible to tap into the part of the soul that is universal, the infinite field of pure potential, and change the course of our destiny. That is synchrodestiny—taking advantage of this connection between the personal soul and the universal soul to shape your life.

So the seeds of memory built by experience, our karma, help determine who we are. But the individuality of our personal soul is shaped by more than karma; our relationships also play an important role in the construction of the soul. Let me explain by more closely examining the different aspects of our existence. When we consider our physical bodies, we discover that we are, really, a collection of recycled molecules. Cells of our body are created, die, and are replaced many times throughout our lives. We are constantly remaking ourselves. In order to regenerate, our bodies convert the food we eat into basic building blocks of life. The earth itself provides the nutrients we need to renew ourselves, and when we shed cells, they are returned to the earth. We might say, then, that we are constantly transforming our physical bodies by recycling earth.

Next, consider our emotions. Emotions are just recycled energy. Emotions do not originate with us. They come and go depending on situations, circumstances, relationships, and events. On September 11, 2001, the date of the World Trade Center disaster, fear and terror were common emotions, triggered by the events of that day. Those powerful emotions continued for months. Emotions are never created in isolation; they always come about because of some interaction with the environment. In the absence of circumstances or relationships, there is no emotion. So even though I may fly into a rage, it is not actually *my* anger. It is anger that has settled on me for the moment.

Think about the last time you were surrounded by people who were all experiencing similar emotions—an angry mob, mourners at a funeral, or fans at a winning soccer match. It is nearly impossible not to get caught up in that emotion because it is so potent when expressed by so many people simultaneously. It would not be "your" anger, sadness, or jubilation, in those situations. Each emotion is dependent on the context, circumstances, and relationships that define your reality at that moment.

And what about our thoughts? Well, our thoughts are recycled information. Every thought we have is actually part of a collective database. One hundred years ago it would have been impossible to say, "I'm going to Disney World on Delta Air Lines." There was no concept of those things in the world at large; therefore I could not have that thought. There was no Disney World, no Delta Air Lines, let alone any commercial air travel. All but the most original thoughts are simply recycled information, and even the most original thoughts are actually quantum leaps of creativity that occur from that same collective, recycled bed of information.

Although the phrase "quantum leap" has become common in everyday conversation, it actually has a very specific meaning. When we are taught about atoms in school, we are usually told that there is a nucleus that contains protons and neutrons, and that electrons circle the nucleus in fixed orbits or shells that are varying distances from the nucleus.

Sodium atom (Na)

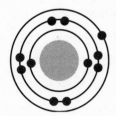

We are told that electrons stay in one particular orbit, but sometimes change to a different orbit. If it absorbs energy, an electron can jump to a higher orbit; if it releases energy, it can drop to a lower orbit. What most of us are never told is that when an electron changes orbits, it does not move through space to arrive at its new location; rather, at one moment the electron is in orbit A, and in the very next moment it is in orbit B, *without having traveled through the space in between.* This is what is meant by a quantum leap. A quantum leap is a change in status from one set of circumstances to another set of circumstances that takes place immediately, without passing through the circumstances in between.

Scientists have learned that they cannot predict when and where a quantum leap will occur. They can create mathematical models that allow them to estimate the quantum leaps, but they are never totally predictable. On a subatomic level, that little bit of unpredictability seems inconsequential. If an electron jumps from orbit to orbit, what does that have to do with me? Well, when we consider all the atoms in the world and all that unpredictability, we're obliged to look at the world in completely new ways.

Scientists recognize the unpredictability of nature, and have been trying to make sense of it. Even the most seemingly simple events are governed by this unpredictability. When and where will bubbles appear in a pot of boiling water? What patterns will be made by the smoke of a lit cigarette? How does the position of water molecules at the top of a waterfall relate to their eventual position at the bottom? As James Gleick wrote in his book *Chaos*, as far as standard physics is concerned, God might just as well have taken all those water molecules under the table and shuffled them personally.

The new science of chaos is attempting to predict the unpredictable through intricate mathematical models. In the classic example, a butterfly flutters its wings in Texas and there is a typhoon in Tokyo six days later. The connection may not seem obvious, but it exists. That little change of air pressure caused by the butterfly can get multiplied and magnified, resulting in a tornado. But it can never be entirely predicted. That's why weather forecasters seem to be wrong so often, and why any forecast longer than about forty-eight hours away is unreliable. Yet among all the possible occurrences in the world, weather is more predictable than just about anything else.

What this says on a spiritual level is that we can never really know what direction life will take, what changes those small butterfly-flutters of intention and action might cause in our destiny. And at the same time, it also tells us that we can never truly know the mind of God. We can never fully understand the how, where, and when of anything, even something as simple as boiling water. We have to surrender to uncertainty, while appreciating its intricate beauty.

All creativity is based on quantum leaps and uncertainty. At particular moments in time, truly novel ideas emanate from the collective bed of information. These ideas did not originate in the fortunate individual, but in the collective consciousness. This is why significant scientific discoveries are often made by two or more different people at the same time. The ideas are already circulating in the collective unconscious, and prepared minds are ready to translate that information. This is the nature of genius, to be able to grasp the knowable even when no one else recognizes that it is present. At any given moment, the innovation or creative idea doesn't exist, and in the next moment, it is part of our conscious world. In between, where was it? It came from the virtual domain, at the level of the universal spirit, where everything is potential. Sometimes this potential creates something predictable, sometimes it creates something novel, but in this realm all possibilities already exist.

So if our bodies are recycled earth, our emotions are recycled energy, and our thoughts are recycled information, what is it that makes you an individual? How about your personality? Well, the personality doesn't originate with us, either. Personality gets created through selective identification with situations and through relationships. Think about a close friend. How do you define that person? Most of us do so by describing the people in their lives—their spouses, their children, their parents, the people they work with. We also describe people in the context of the situations in their lives, what kinds of jobs they perform, where they live, what they do for fun. What we call personality is built on a foundation of relationships and situations.

So now we may ask, if my body, emotions, thoughts, and personality are not original or created by me, who am I really? According to many of the great spiritual traditions, one of the great truths is that "I am the other." Without the other, we would not exist. Your soul is the reflection of all souls. Imagine trying to understand the complex web of personal interactions that have made you who you are today—all your family and friends, every teacher and classmate you've ever had, every shop clerk in every store you've ever visited, everyone you've ever worked with or come in contact with at any point in your life. And then, in order to understand all those people and the type of influence they may have had on you, you have to find out who *they* are. So now you have to describe the web of relationships surrounding every one of those people who form your relationship network. Eventually, you would find that you would need to describe the whole universe in order to define a single person. In truth, then, every single person *is* the whole universe. You are the infinite, seen from a specific, localized point of view. Your soul is the part of you that is universal and individual at the same time, and it is a reflection of all other souls.

To define the soul in this way, therefore, is to understand that your soul is both personal and universal at the same time, which has meaning and implications beyond your personal experience of life. The soul is the observer who interprets and makes choices in a confluence of relationships. These relationships provide the background, setting, characters, and events that shape the stories of our lives. Just as the soul is created through relationships and is a reflection of all relationships, the experience of life is created from context and meaning.

By *context* I mean everything that surrounds us that allows us to understand the meaning of individual actions, words, occurrences, or anything else. A word, for example, can have different meanings depending on what surrounds it, or its context. If I say the word "bark" without context, you won't know whether I mean the bark of a dog or the bark of a tree. When we say that someone took our words "out of context," we know that the meaning of our words was misunderstood, because context determines the meaning of everything. The flow of meaning is the flow of life. Our context determines how we will interpret what we encounter in life, and these interpretations become our experience.

Finally, we come to a more complete definition of a soul. *A soul is the observer who interprets and makes choices based on karma; it is also a confluence of relationships, out of which emerge contexts and meaning, and it is this flow of context and meaning that creates experience.* So it is through the soul that we create our lives.

As I will discuss later, the best way to approach an understanding of the dual nature of the soul and to tap into the nonlocal field of potential is through meditation. Meditation allows us to reach the level of the soul by easing past the tangle of thoughts and emotions that usually keep our attention bound to the physical world. When we close our eyes to meditate, thoughts spring up spontaneously. There are only two kinds of thoughts you can have, memories and imaginings. But, as we've discussed, these thoughts do not originate in your physical body.

Try this little thought experiment: Think about the dinner you ate last night. Can you remember what you were eating? What the food tasted like? What conversations were going on around you? Now, where was that information before I asked those questions? That dinner took place, but the information about it didn't exist except as potential information. If a surgeon went inside your brain, there would be no trace of information about the food you ate for dinner. Memory resides at the level of the soul until we call it up. Once we consciously decide to recall our dinner, electrical activity and a release of chemicals signal that the brain is at work. But before we pull up the memory, it has no location in your brain. Simply asking a question or trying to recall an event converts a virtual memory into a real memory.

The same is true of imagination. Until a thought arises from the virtual realm, it does not exist in your mental or physical life. But imagination can have a powerful effect on the mind and body. A common but highly effective thought experiment is to imagine slicing a lemon into large wedges, putting a wedge between your teeth, and biting into the flesh of the lemon. Imagine the juice squirting into your mouth as you bite down. If you are like most people, just that quick thought led to a rush of saliva in your mouth, your body's way of saying that it believes what your mind is telling it. But again, where was that lemon before I asked you to think of it? It did not exist anywhere but at the level of potential.

So intention, imagination, insight, intuition, inspiration, meaning, purpose, creativity, understanding, all these have nothing to do with the brain. They orchestrate their activity *through* the brain, but they are qualities of the nonlocal domain, which is beyond space and time. Still, their impact is felt very strongly. Once they enter our minds, we have to do something with them, and what we do with them determines, in part, who you define yourself to be. That's because we have rational minds, and we tend to create stories around these thoughts. You might think, "My husband loves me," or "My children are happy," or "I enjoy my work." You create rational stories around these thoughts, and then you create meaning out of them. Then you go and live out these stories in the physical world, and this is what we call everyday life.

Our stories are derived from relationships, contexts, and meanings triggered through memory, arising from karma and experience. As we live out these stories, we start to realize that they are not original. Although the details of the stories vary from individual to individual, the themes and motifs are timeless, basic archetypes that replay endlessly: heroes and villains; sin and redemption; the divine and the diabolical; forbidden lust and unconditional love. These are the same themes that keep many of us fascinated by soap operas, gossip columns, and tabloids, where we see them expressed in slightly exaggerated form. We're fascinated because we can identify some aspect of our souls in those stories. These are the same archetypes that are represented in exaggerated form in mythologies, so whether we examine Indian mythology or Greek mythology or Egyptian mythology, we find these same themes and motifs. The drama of these stories is more compelling and more dramatic than fiction because they resonate in our soul.

So now we can refine our definition of the soul even further. *The soul is the confluence of meanings, contexts, relationships, and mythical stories or archetypal themes that give rise to everyday thoughts, memories, and desires (conditioned by karma) that create the stories in which we participate.*

In nearly everyone, this participation in the stories of our lives is happening automatically, without awareness. We live like actors in a play who are given only one line at a time, going through the motions without understanding the full story. But when you get in touch with your soul, you see the whole script for the drama. You understand. You still participate in the story, but now you participate joyously, consciously, and fully. You can make choices based on knowledge and born out of freedom. Each moment takes on a deeper quality that comes from appreciation of what it means in the context of your life.

What is even more thrilling is that we, ourselves, are capable of rewriting the play or changing our roles by applying intention, grasping the opportunities that arise from coincidence, and being true to the calling of our souls.

Intention

4

Every child who has ever heard the story of Aladdin dreams of finding a magic lamp that, when rubbed, would deliver a genie who could grant every wish. As adults, we understand that there are no such lamps and no such genies, which leaves all those wishes bottled up inside us. But what if wishes could come true? What wishes would you make for yourself? What would fulfill your needs at the deepest, most basic level? What would allow your soul to complete its destiny?

Everything that happens in the universe starts with intention. When I decide to wiggle my toes, or buy a birthday present for my wife, or drink a cup of coffee, or write this book, it all starts with intention. This intention always arises in the nonlocal or universal mind, but it localizes through the individual mind. And having localized, it becomes physical reality.

In fact, physical reality would not exist were it not for intent. Intent activates nonlocal, synchronized correlation in the brain. Whenever there is cognition or perception of physical reality, the brain's disparate regions show a "phase and frequency locking in" of the firing patterns of individual neurons in different parts of the brain. This is nonlocal synchronization around a frequency of forty hertz (forty cycles per second). This synchronization, also called binding, is a requirement for cognition. Without it you would not see a person as a person, a house as a house, a tree as a tree, or a face in a photograph as a face. You might just observe dots of black and white, scattered lines, patches of light and dark. In fact, the objects of your perception register only as on-off electromagnetic signals in your brain. Synchronization organized by intent converts dots and spots, scattered lines, electrical discharges, patterns of light and darkness, into a wholeness, a gestalt that creates a picture of the world as a subjective experience. The world does not exist as pictures, but only as these patches of on-off impulses, these dots and spots, these digital codes of seemingly random electrical firings. Synchronization through intent organizes them into an experience in the brain—a sound, a texture, a form, a taste, and a smell. You as nonlocal intelligence "label" that experience and suddenly there is the creation of a material object in subjective consciousness.

The world is like a Rorschach blot that we convert into a world of material objects through synchronization orchestrated by intent. The world before it is observed and the nervous system before the desire or intent to observe something both exist as a dynamic (constantly changing), nonlinear chaotic field of activities in a state of non-equilibrium (unstable activity). Intent synchronistically organizes these highly variable, seemingly chaotic and unrelated activities in a nonlocal universe into a highly ordered, self-organizing, dynamic system that manifests simultaneously as an observed world and a nervous system through which that world is being observed. The intent itself does not arise in the nervous system, although it is orchestrated through the nervous system. However, intent is responsible for more than cognition and perception. All learning, remembering, reasoning, drawing of inferences, and motor activity are preceded by intent. Intent is the very basis of creation.

The ancient Vedic texts known as the Upanishads declare, "You are what your deepest desire is. As is your desire, so is your intention. As is your intention, so is your will. As is your will, so is your deed. As is your deed, so is your destiny." Our destiny ultimately comes from the deepest level of desire and also from the deepest level of intention. The two are intimately linked to each other.

What *is* intention? Most people say it's a thought of something that you want to accomplish in your life or that you want for yourself. But really it is more than that. An intention is a way of fulfilling a certain need that you have, whether that need is for material things, for a relationship, for spiritual fulfillment, or for love. Intention is a thought that you have that will help you to fulfill a need. And the logic is that once you fulfill that need, you will be happy.

Seen this way, the goal of all our intentions is to be happy or fulfilled. First, if we are asked what we want, we might say, "I want more money," or "I want a new relationship." Then if we are asked why we want that, we may say something like, "Well, so I'll be to spend more time with my children." If we are asked why we want to spend more time with our children, we might say, "Because then I'll be happy." So we can see that the ultimate goal of all goals is a fulfillment at the spiritual level that we call happiness or joy or love.

All the activity in the universe is generated by intention. According to Vedantic tradition, "Intent is a force of nature." Intent maintains the balance of all the universal elements and forces that allow the universe to continue to evolve.

Even creativity is orchestrated through intent. Creativity occurs at the individual level, but it also occurs universally, allowing the world to periodically take quantum leaps in evolution. Ultimately, when we die, the soul takes a quantum leap in creativity. In effect it says, "I now must express myself through a new body-mind system, or incarnation." So intent comes from the universal soul, becomes localized in an individual soul, and is finally expressed through an individual, local mind.

From experience in the past we create memories, which are the basis of imagination and desire. Desire is the basis of action, once again. And so the cycle perpetuates itself. In Vedic tradition and in Buddhism this cycle is known as the Wheel of Samsara, the basis of earthly existence. The nonlocal "I" becomes the local "I" as it filters through this karmic process.

When intention is repeated, that creates habit. The more an intention is repeated, the more likely it is that the universal consciousness will create the same pattern and manifest the intention in the physical world. If you recall the physics discussion earlier, a wave-particle in an unobserved box is simultaneously a wave and a particle, and takes on definite shape only once it is observed. At the moment of observation, the probability collapses into a definite form. This is the same idea, only with repeated intention the pattern in the nonlocal mind is more likely to collapse in the direction of your intention and therefore will manifest as physical reality. This creates the illusion of what is easy and what is difficult, what is possible and what is impossible. That's why, if you really want to break out of the mundane, you must learn to think and dream the impossible. Only with repeated thoughts can the impossible be made possible through the intention of the nonlocal mind.

The nonlocal mind in you is the same as the nonlocal mind in me, or, in fact, in a rhinoceros or in a giraffe or in a bird or in a worm. Even a rock contains nonlocal intelligence. This nonlocal mind, this pure consciousness, is what gives us the sense of "I," the "I" that says "I am Deepak," the "I" that says "I'm a bird," the "I" that says who you are or who you believe you are. This universal consciousness is the only "I" there is. But that single, universal "I" differentiates; it morphs itself into an almost infinite number of observers and observed, seers and scenery, organic forms and inorganic forms—all the beings and objects that make up the physical world. This habit of the universal consciousness to differentiate into particular consciousnesses exists prior to interpretation. So, before the "I am" says "I am Deepak," or a giraffe, or a worm, it is simply "I am." The infinite creative potential of the "I" organizes the communal "I" into the "I" that is you, or me, or any other thing in the universe.

This is the same concept as the two levels of the soul, the universal soul and the individual soul, but put into a personal context. As human beings, we are used to thinking of our individual selves as "I," without noticing or appreciating the greater, universal "I" that is also called the universal soul. The use of the word "I" is merely a clever reference point we use for locating our unique point of view within the universal soul. But when we define ourselves solely as an individual "I," we lose the ability to imagine beyond the boundaries of what is traditionally considered possible. In the universal "I," everything is not only possible, it already exists, and simply requires intent to collapse it into a reality in the physical world.

The differences between the individual "I" or local mind and the universal "I" or nonlocal mind can be clearly seen in the following chart:

Local Mind

1. ego mind

2. individual mind

3. individual consciousness

4. conditioned consciousness

5. linear

6. operates within space, time, causality

7. time-bound and limited

8. rational

9. conditioned into habitual ways of thinking and behavior, shaped by individual and collective experience

10. separates

11. inner dialogue: *This is me and mine*

12. fear dominates

Nonlocal Mind

1. spirit

2. soul

3. universal consciousness

4. pure consciousness

5. synchronistic

6. operates outside space, time, causality

7. timeless and infinite

8. intuitive/creative

9. unconditioned, infinitely correlated, infinitely creative

10. unifies

11. inner dialogue: All this is me and mine

12. love dominates

Local Mind

13. *requires energy*

14. *needs approval*

15. *interprets the "I" within the observer as different from the "I" in the observed*

16. *thinks in cause-and-effect modalities*

17. *algorithmic*

18. *continuous*

19. *conscious*

20. *active when senses are active because sensory experience is local*

21. *expresses itself through the voluntary nervous system (individual choice)*

13. *operates without energy*

14. *immune to criticism and flattery*

15. *knows it is the same "I" in the observer and the observed*

16. *sees an acausal interconnectedness or interdependent correlation*

17. *nonalgorithmic*

18. *discontinuous*

19. *supra-conscious*

20. *always active, but more available to itself when senses are in abeyance or withdrawn, as in sleep, dreams, meditation, drowsiness, trance, prayer*

21. *expresses itself through autonomic and endocrine systems, and, most important, through the synchronization of these systems (and also through the synchronization of the particular and the universal, the microcosm and the macrocosm)*

The difference between local mind and nonlocal mind is the difference between ordinary and extraordinary. The local mind is personal and individual to each of us. It holds our ego, the self-defined "I" that wanders through the world a slave to our conditioned habits. By its very nature, the local mind separates us from the rest of creation. It puts up thick, artificial boundaries that many of us feel compelled to defend, even when this means cutting ourselves off from the deeper meanings and joyous connections that come from feeling part of the universal. Local mind is plodding, exhausting, and rational, with no sense of whimsy or creativity. It requires constant attention and approval, and is therefore prone to fear, disappointment, and pain.

Nonlocal mind, on the other hand, is pure soul or spirit, known as universal consciousness. Operating outside the boundaries of normal space and time, it is the great organizing and unifying force in the universe, infinite in scope and duration. By its nature, nonlocal mind connects all things because it *is* all things. It requires no attention, no energy, no approval; it is whole unto itself, and therefore attracts love and acceptance. It is imminently creative, the source from which all creation flows. It allows us to imagine beyond the boundaries of what local mind sees as "possible," to think "outside the box," and to believe in miracles.

The creative leaps taken by nonlocal mind have

been supported by science. Gaps in the fossil record during evolution suggest creative leaps of imagination in nature itself, a hypothesis known as punctuated equilibrium. For example, there are ancient fossils of amphibians, and ancient fossils of birds, but there is no fossil record of a connecting creature between amphibians and birds. That suggests a quantum leap of imagination, where amphibians wanted to learn how to fly, and birds manifested as a result of that intent. Scientists believe primates evolved into humans, but there is no fossil record of the phase in between, the "missing link." First there were only primates, and then suddenly human beings appeared. In between? Nothing.

These leaps of imagination are constantly evolving into what we see as the universe. In our lifetime, we've seen the development of television, the Internet, e-mail, nuclear technology, and space exploration. Imagination leads wherever we go. And although imagination is a property of the universal consciousness, it gets conditioned through all these localized expressions. Human beings have the ability to go beyond that. They have the ability, through the local mind, the local "I," to make choices through intention. And the nonlocal mind, the nonlocal "I," takes care of the details synchronistically to fulfill the intention. That is how dreams become reality.

Let me explain this with an example. The local "I," which is Deepak, wants to feel good by exercising and losing weight. So, Deepak, the local "I," goes running every day, either on the treadmill or by the beach. The nonlocal "I" in Deepak makes this possible by making Deepak's body perform many functions simultaneously: The heart has to beat faster and pump more blood, the tissues have to consume more oxygen, the lungs have to breathe faster and deeper, and the sugar, which is the fuel in my system, has to quickly burn into carbon dioxide and water so that energy can be generated. If the fuel supply gets low, then insulin has to be secreted so that glycogen stored in the liver can be used as fuel. Immune cells have to be stimulated so the body mind becomes resistant to infection as I'm running through the environment. This is only a very abbreviated list of things that must happen simultaneously and synchronistically so that my intention to run can be fulfilled. In fact, trillions upon trillions of activities have to happen nonlocally, simultaneously, in order for Deepak to enjoy running.

As we can see, the operation of the body is being organized by the nonlocal mind. And while all these activities are being synchronized, Deepak is enjoying his run. He's not worrying about whether his heart will pump the right amount of blood, or whether his liver will forget to metabolize glycogen into sugar. That's the job of nonlocal intelligence. The local "I" intends, and the nonlocal "I" organizes all the details synchronistically.

But the local "I" does not always cooperate, and sometimes makes bad decisions. Imagine a man named Jim Smith. He's at a party and the local Jim Smith says, "I'm having a good time at this party." He sips a little champagne, loosens up, and makes new friends. The nonlocal Jim Smith at the party is also having fun, connecting and enjoying the moment. But what if the local "I" says, "This is a lot of fun. Maybe I should drink more and get drunk." Getting drunk is a way of disconnecting; therefore the nonlocal "I" lets the local "I" know that that decision has a price. The nonlocal "I" gives the local "I" a headache and a hangover the next morning. This is its way of communicating with the local "I," saying in effect, If you abuse yourself, you'll get sick.

If the local "I" ignores the nonlocal "I" in its efforts to dissuade it from that decision, it will face worse repercussions. If, for example, the local "I" ignores that message and gets drunk every day, then the local Jim Smith might lose his job, lose his income, disrupt his family relationships, and perhaps get cirrhosis of the liver and eventually die. Why? Because the decision to drink was not serving the interests of both the local and the nonlocal Jim Smiths. It was not a pure intention because the local "I" warped it. It changed form as it moved from the nonlocal mind to the local mind. An intention can be fulfilled synchronistically only if it serves the needs of both the local and the nonlocal "I." The nonlocal intention is always evolutionary and therefore moving in the direction of harmonious interactions that serve the larger good.

Intention always originates in the universal domain. Ultimately, it is universal intention that fulfills the local intention, as long as it serves the needs of the local mind (me) and the nonlocal mind (the universal spirit). Only then will both local and nonlocal minds cooperate. But there is a confounding factor at play. There are billions of human beings and trillions of other entities on earth, all with local intentions. Let's say I'm going to have a party, and I plan to bake lots of pastries and lots of cakes. In preparation I have bought sugar, flour, and all the other items that I need. All of this is stored in my pantry, where it attracts ants and mice, whose intention is to consume the sugar and the flour, too. When I discover the activity of the mice, I buy rat traps and insecticide. Some of the mice die. Bacteria arrive and start breaking down their bodies.

If we step back and take a wider look at this scenario, we see a conspiracy of related events. They all co-arose and co-created each other. In order for this drama to occur, wheat and sugarcane must be grown. That involves farms, farmers, rainfall, sunshine, tractors, consumers, retailers, wholesalers, truckers, railroads, financial trading markets, grocery stores and their employees, investors, insecticides, chemical factories, knowledge of chemistry, and on and on. The number of individual local minds involved is enormous.

The question might fairly be asked, then, Who is influencing what? Whose intention is creating the events? My intention was to bake pastries and cakes. Is my intent influencing the behavior of the entire planet, from farmers to stock market analysts to wheat prices—not to mention the behavior of the ants and mice in my pantry, and the activities of other elements and forces in the universe? Was my intent to serve pastries and cakes the only intent in which the whole universe has to cooperate? A mouse, assuming it was able to consider its intent, might believe that its intent was responsible for creating this series of events, from the activity of grain traders to weather conditions to my decision to make cakes. In fact, the bacteria could just as easily believe that their intent orchestrated the activity of the whole universe, including my decision to buy the poison that created the protein for their consumption. It can seem very confusing when you start to ask whose intent orchestrated any given event.

Whose intent *is* creating all this activity? In the deeper reality, the "I" that orchestrates all these events is the nonlocal, universal "I." This organizing force is coordinating and synchronizing an infinite number of events simultaneously. The nonlocal mind constantly turns back into itself, renews itself and its creativity, so that the old never gets stale but is born afresh every moment. Even though intent comes from the single non-local "I," from my perspective and that of the cat, the mouse, the ants, the bacteria, and the people who are coming to the party, it appears to be the intent of a personal "I."

At every location, every organism could be thinking "It's my intent!" Each and every one believes it is their personal local "I" that is doing something, but in the larger scheme, all these different local minds are actually co-arising and co-creating each other, through the intent of the nonlocal mind. The trees must breathe so I can breathe. The rivers must flow so that my blood can circulate. In the end, there's only one exuberant, abundant, eternal, rhythmic, inseparable "I." All separation is illusion. The local "I" only realizes itself as the nonlocal "I" when the two connect. Then you start to sense that there's only one universal "I." And when you connect, you start to experience trust, love, forgiveness, gratitude, compassion, surrender, nondoing. This is how prayer works. The great poet Alfred, Lord Tennyson, once said, "More things are wrought by prayer than this world dreams of." But it's not prayer through forced intent; it's finesse, timing, surrender, gratitude, trust, love, and compassion that allow me, the local "I," to experience and become the nonlocal "I."

We are so attached to our local, individual, personal "I" that we are blinded to the magnificence that lies beyond it. Ignorance is constricted awareness. In order to notice something, you have to ignore everything else. That's how nonlocal becomes local. When I notice anything, I ignore everything else around it, which nevertheless contributes to its existence and is therefore a part of it. When the "I" that is my ego observes, it observes only the particular and ignores the universal. But when "I" the spirit sees, it sees the flow of the universe that makes the particular possible.

It is this interconnection, this inseparability, that makes life not only possible, but miraculous. The world's sea of interrelatedness collapses into individual waves that scatter into foaming drops that sparkle like diamonds, reflecting one another for a moment, only to subside back into the ocean's depths. There is only one eternal moment—an eternal love, spirit, or consciousness—that constantly becomes seer and scenery. We are those crystalline drops, each of us beautiful and unique for a moment, each a part of the other, each reflecting the other. We all derive from eternal love, spirit, or consciousness, an imagining of the universal "I." While interpretation, memory, and habit create the illusion of familiarity or sameness, of our continuation from minute to minute, in reality, there are infinite possibilities at our core, infinite possibilities that need only intent to make them real.

Intention orchestrates infinite possibilities. You might wonder what kind of intent is ideal. What would you ask if your intention could be fulfilled right now? If your intent is a mere personal wish, and serves only personal gratification, the local and nonlocal "I" might be out of sync. How many times have you heard people wish they might win the lottery? It might happen, but only if the fulfillment of that intention serves both you and the larger purpose. You might say to yourself, "I want to win the lottery so I can get myself a new BMW." Even that intention serves many people: you, the car manufacturer, its employees, investors, and the economy. However, it is not as powerful as the intent of someone like Mother Teresa, because her desire to raise money was the result of a desire to bring fulfillment to others, to give and receive at a deeper level—to serve the great chain of being. When the intention of the nonlocal mind is served by the local mind, it is more holistic, and therefore more effective.

For every intention, we might well ask, "How would this serve me and how would it serve everybody I come into contact with?" And if the answer is that it will create true joy and fulfillment in me and all those affected by my actions, then my intention, together with surrender to the nonlocal mind, orchestrates its own fulfillment. There are techniques for discovering the pure and proper intention that is your life's destiny, which we will discuss in detail later on. But the core technique is to start from a place of quiet and settled awareness, to create a proper intention in your heart, and then to let your local "I" merge back into the nonlocal "I," allowing the will of God to be completed through you. I have taught this technique to many thousands of people and they tell me that it works for them, as it works for me.

Part of the difficulty is forming an intention that doesn't interfere with the intention of the universal. In developing countries with a food shortage, scientists recently attempted to introduce "golden rice," a genetically engineered variant that contains natural insecticides so that the rice grows abundantly. But there were problems. The genetically engineered rice doesn't have natural odors that attract various insects important for maintaining and propagating the food chain. Ecologists fear that this rice might upset the local ecosystem, eventually disrupting the weather, which could have dire consequences for the entire planet. Constricted or local awareness, looking only at a particular situation, tries to solve it locally. Expanded awareness, the nonlocal "I," looks at the relationships, the birds, the bees, the squirrels, the groundhogs, and the weather (there has to be a given population of trees and flora and fauna to enable a certain type of weather to arise). A good intention can backfire if the intent of the nonlocal "I" is ignored. The intricate bonds of interconnection require not only selflessness but coordination with all other individual "I"s that stem from the universal "I."

Intent cannot be pushed or forced or bullied.

Think of it as catching soap bubbles in the air. It is a delicate endeavor that cannot be rushed or pushed. The same is true of meditation or sleep. One cannot *try* to meditate or sleep. These activities require letting go, and the harder you try, the less successful you will be. Meditation happens; sleep happens. It is the same with intention. The less we interfere with it, the more we see that it has its own "infinite organizing power." Intent has within it the mechanisms for its own fulfillment, like a seed has within it everything it needs to become the tree, the flower, and the fruit. I don't have to do anything with that seed. I just have to put it in the ground and water it. The seed itself, without any prompting from me, will create everything thereafter.

Intent is a seed in consciousness, or spirit. If you pay attention to it, it has within it the means for its own fulfillment. Intention's infinite organizing power orchestrates countless details simultaneously.

Intent creates coincidences; it is the reason why, when you're thinking of something, it happens. Intent is the reason why some people have a spontaneous remission or heal themselves. Intent orchestrates all the creativity in the universe. And we, as human beings, are capable of creating positive changes in our lives through intent. So why do we lose that ability? The ability is lost when the self-image overshadows the self, when we sacrifice our true self for the ego.

The realization that "I" am separate from "you" starts to happen at around age two or three. At this stage a baby starts to differentiate between "me" and "mine," and "not me" and "not mine." This separation creates anxiety. In reality the world is not separate from us, but part of the continuum of consciousness. Intent works by harnessing the creative forces inherent in the universe. Just as we have our personal creativity, the universe also displays creativity. The universe is alive and conscious, and it responds to our intent when we have our intimate relationship with the universe and see it not as separate but as our extended body.

We can restore the power of intent through a return to the true self, or self-actualization. People who attain self-actualization reestablish their connectedness to the nonlocal mind. They have no desire to manipulate and control others. They are independent of criticism and also of flattery. They feel beneath no one, but they also feel superior to no one. They are in touch with the internal reference point that is their soul, and not their ego. Anxiety is no longer an issue, because anxiety comes from the ego's need to protect itself. And that anxiety is what interferes with the spontaneity of intent. Intent is the mechanics through which spirit transforms itself into material reality.

Mature spirituality requires sobriety of awareness. If you are sober, you are responsive to feedback but at the same time immune to criticism and flattery. You learn to let go and you do not worry about the result. You have confidence in the outcome, and you start to see the synchronicity that is always organized around you. Intention provides opportunities that you have to be alert to. Good luck is opportunity and preparedness coming together. Intention will provide you opportunities, but you still need to act when the opportunity is provided.

Whenever you take action, have the attitude that you are not performing the action. Have the attitude that your actions are really the actions of nonlocal intelligence, the organizing universal spirit. You will begin to notice a great diminution of anxiety. You will also be less attached to the result.

Stress is a form of anxiety. If you're stressed, then you can't even begin to think about synchronicity. Synchronicity is a means of getting in touch with God. It's a path to meaning and purpose in your life. It's a means of having the experience of love and compassion. It's a means of connecting to the nonlocal intelligence of the universe. If my attention is on situations that generate stress, then it is difficult to access synchronicity. To do so effectively you have to have an attitude of surrender to the universal domain, which is much grander than anything you could imagine. Surrender requires a leap of faith, a jump into the unknown. Your inner dialogue can support this by saying, "Things are not going my way. I'm letting go of my idea of how they should. My sense of 'me and mine' has to expand." If you take this leap of faith, you will be richly rewarded. If you find yourself worrying about next month's bills, it would be appropriate to remind yourself that it is your intent not only to fulfill your needs but also to send your children to school, to contribute to your community. All people want to fulfill these needs in their lives. However, having articulated and expressed your intent to fulfill them takes them to the infinite mind, and in effect says, "I put all this at your disposal. I'm not going to worry about it because you, the nonlocal intelligence that resides within me, will take care of it."

Great artists, jazz musicians, writers, and scientists talk about having to transcend their individual identities when they create. I've worked with a lot of musicians and songwriters and I've never known any who are thinking about royalties when they are writing a song. A new song or a new piece of music involves letting go, and incubating in the nonlocal domain, then allowing the music or song to come to you. All creative processes depend on a phase of incubation and allowing. Synchronization is a creative process. In this case, however, the creative mind is the cosmos itself. When self-concern departs, nonlocal intelligence enters.

Remember, your thoughts must not conflict with the designs of the universe. Wishing to win the lottery can magnify your sense of separation from the universe. Frequently lottery winners report alienation from friends and family and no greater happiness. When money alone becomes the goal, it alienates you.

How do you know which of your intentions is likely to be fulfilled? The answer lies in paying attention to the clues provided by the nonlocal mind. Notice the coincidences in your life. Coincidences are messages. They are clues from God or spirit or nonlocal reality, urging you to break out of your karmic conditioning, your familiar patterns of thinking. They are offering you an opportunity to enter a domain of awareness where you feel loved and cared for by the infinite intelligence that is your source. Spiritual traditions call this the state of grace.

The Role of Coincidence

5

To talk about coincidences as coded messages from the nonlocal intelligence makes life sound like a mystery novel. Pay attention, watch for clues, decipher their meanings, and eventually the truth will be revealed. In many ways, that's exactly what happens. After all, life is the ultimate mystery.

What makes life mysterious is that our destiny seems hidden from us, and only at the end of our lives will we be in a position to look back and see the path we followed. In retrospect, the narrative of our lives appears perfectly logical. We can easily follow the thread of continuity upon which we gathered our life's experiences. Even now, at whatever point you are in your life, look back and notice how naturally your life flowed from one milestone to the next, from one place or job to another, from one set of circumstances to an entirely different set. Notice how effortless it all could have been if you had only known where your path was leading. Most people look back and ask, What was I so worried about? Why was I so hard on myself, or on my children?

If we were able to live at the level of the soul all the time, there would be no need for hindsight to appreciate the great truths of life. We would know them in advance. We would participate in creating the adventures of our lives. The path would be clearly marked, and we would need no signposts, no clues, and no coincidences.

Most of us don't live at the level of the soul, however, so we must depend on coincidences to show us the will of the universe. We have all experienced coincidences in our lives. The word itself perfectly describes its meaning: *co* means "with," and *incidence* means "event." So the word *coincidence* refers to events or incidents that occur *with* other incidents—two or more events occurring at the same time. Because the experience of coincidences is universal, most people take them for granted, life's little quirky moments that we marvel over, then quickly forget.

Coincidences are so much more than amuse-
ments. A coincidence is a clue to the intention of
the universal spirit, and as such it is rich with significance. Some people use the phrase "meaningful coincidence" to describe events happening at
the same time that have some special meaning for
the person who experienced them. But I believe
"meaningful coincidence" is redundant because
every coincidence is meaningful; otherwise it
would not happen in the first place. The very fact
that it happens is meaningful. It's just that sometimes we are able to glimpse its meaning and
sometimes we aren't.

What *is* the meaning in a coincidence? The
deeper part of you already knows, but that awareness has to be brought to the surface. The meaning does not come from the coincidence itself. It
comes from you, the person who is having the
experience. In fact, without our participation any
incident is essentially meaningless, the whole universe is meaningless. We are the ones who give
meaning to events, and we give meaning to events
through intention. Coincidences are messages
from the nonlocal realm, guiding us in the ways to
act in order to make our dreams, our intentions
manifest. So first you must have an intention, and
then you must get in touch with your spiritual
self. Only then will you have a way of using coincidence to fulfill your intentions.

Having an intention is easy; it's as simple as making a wish for one's life. Becoming more spiritual

is difficult. Many people who believe themselves to be spiritual are still not tapping into the vast ocean of the spirit force. Rather, they swim across the surface of that ocean, never diving to discover the depths of the universal experience.

MIRACLES IN THE REAL WORLD

Miracles are real phenomena. Every tradition addresses the existence of miracles, but they all use different language. We label events as miracles when a desired outcome manifests in a dramatic fashion: We want to be healed from a terrible illness, or attain material wealth, or find our purpose. Then when these events occur, we say, how miraculous! Someone has an intention or a desire or a thought, and then it happens. A miracle, then, is a very dramatic example of what happens when a person is able to tap into the spiritual domain and apply intention to manifest their destiny.

Let me give you an example of a remarkable coincidence. David was in love with a woman named Joanna. He was utterly in love, but a little tentative about commitment and marriage. He finally decided that he would take Joanna to a park and propose to her. He was still leery of commitment, but when he awoke that morning he felt overcome by a feeling of peace, a sense that all would be well. David set out the picnic blanket and was just getting up the nerve to pop the question when a plane flew overhead trailing an advertising banner. Joanna looked up and said, "I wonder what that banner says." Without thinking David blurted out, "The banner says, 'Joanna, marry me.'" They both looked more closely, and there indeed was a banner that read, JOANNA, MARRY ME. She fell into his arms, they kissed, and at that moment David knew that marrying her was exactly right for him. The next day, they read in the local newspaper that someone else had proposed to his girlfriend, Joanna, with a banner over the park; the plane just happened to be overhead at exactly the right moment for David. This remarkable coincidence was a clue to David's future, a miracle. The two remain happily married to this day.

People who are not interested in spirituality attribute these kinds of events to luck. I personally believe that "luck"—at least the way we usually define it—has nothing to do with it. What most people call luck is nothing more or less than the application of synchronicity to the fulfillment of our intentions. Louis Pasteur, the scientist who discovered that microbes can cause disease, said, "Chance favors the prepared mind." This can be converted into a simple equation: Opportunity + Preparedness = Good Luck. It is entirely possible, through the lessons of synchrondestiny, to create such a state of mind that you will begin to see that there are opportune moments in life, and when you notice and take hold of them, they change everything. "Luck" is the word we in the modern world use to describe the miraculous.

So synchronicity, meaningful coincidence, miracles, good luck—these are all different terms for the same phenomenon. As we have seen, the intelligence of the body works through coincidence and synchronicity. The extended intelligence of nature and the ecosystem, the great web of life, also works through coincidence and synchronicity, as does the fundamental intelligence of the universe.

When you begin seeing coincidences as life opportunities, every coincidence becomes meaningful. Every coincidence becomes an opportunity for creativity. Every coincidence becomes an opportunity for you to become the person the universe intended you to be.

This is the ultimate truth of synchrodestiny— that the sum total of the universe is conspiring to create your personal destiny. To do so it uses "*acausal* nonlocal connections." What are acausal connections? If we look at all the disparate incidents in our lives very deeply, they all have a history woven together with a personal destiny. *Acausal* means that the incidents are connected to each other, yet without a direct cause-and-effect relationship, at least on the surface. They are *acausal*, from a Latin phrase meaning "without cause." Going back to the example I mentioned in the first chapter, what does Lady Mountbatten liking my father have to do with my reading Sinclair Lewis, or my being inspired by my best friend, Oppo? There is no connection, other than that they are all part of my history, which led me to my particular destiny. Not one of those events *caused* the other events to occur. Lady Mountbatten did not order my father to give me a Sinclair Lewis book, and yet those two incidents worked together to shape my destiny. They were all connected at a deeper level.

We cannot even imagine the complex forces behind every event that occurs in our lives. There's a conspiracy of coincidences that weaves the web of karma or destiny and creates an individual's personal life—mine, or yours. The only reason we don't experience synchronicity in our daily lives is that we do not live from the level where it is happening. Usually we see only cause-and-effect relationships: This causes that, which causes this, which causes that—linear trajectories. Yet beneath the surface, something else is happening. Invisible to us is a whole web of connections. As it becomes apparent, we see how our intentions are woven into this web, which is much more context-bound, much more relational, much more holistic, much more nurturing than our surface experience.

Very often we fall into ruts in our lives; we maintain the same routines and act in the same manner predictably day after day after day. We set our minds on a certain course of action, and simply proceed. How can miracles happen if we march mindlessly, unthinking and unaware, through our lives? Coincidences are like road flares, calling our attention to something important in our lives, glimpses of what goes on beyond everyday distractions. We can choose to ignore those flares and hurry on, or we can pay attention to them and live out the miracle that is waiting for us.

When I was finishing my medical training, I knew that my interest was in neuro-endocrinology, the study of how brain chemicals work. Even then, I could see that this was a place where science and consciousness met, and I wanted to explore it. I applied for a fellowship to train with one of the world's most prominent endocrinologists. This highly respected scientist was doing Nobel Prize–worthy work, and I was eager for the opportunity to learn from him. Out of thousands of applicants, I was one of six selected to work with him that year. Shortly after I started, I realized that his laboratory was more about ego gratification than about real science. We technicians were treated like machines, expected to mass-produce publishable research papers. It was tedious and unsatisfying. And it was terribly disillusioning to work with someone so famous, so respected, and still manage to feel as unhappy as I did. I had taken the position with such idealism, and I found myself doing nothing but injecting rats with chemicals all day long.

Every morning I scanned the *Boston Globe* newspaper want ads, aware of my disappointment, but thinking that this path I was on was the only way to go. I remember reading a little advertisement for a position in a local hospital emergency room. In fact, every day when I opened the newspaper, I would see that little ad. Even if I was only flipping through the paper quickly, it would fall open to that same page with that same ad. I would look at it and then push it out of my mind. Deep inside, I could imagine myself working in the emergency room and actually helping people, instead of injecting chemicals into rats, but my dream had been to land this fellowship with the renowned endocrinologist.

One day that endocrinologist addressed me in a cruel and demeaning manner. We argued, and I walked away to the lounge to calm myself down. On the table was the *Boston Globe* newspaper, opened to the page with the little want ad—that same ad that I had ignored for weeks. The coincidence was too powerful to ignore. Everything finally clicked into place. I knew I was in the wrong place doing the wrong thing. I was fed up with the routine, with the ego of that endocrinologist, with the rats, with the feeling that I was not doing what was in my heart to do. I walked back into his office and quit. He followed me out into the parking lot, screaming at the top of his lungs that my career was ruined, that he would see to it that no one would ever hire me.

With his voice still ringing in my ears, I drove directly to that little emergency room, applied for the position, and started work that very day. For the first time, I got to treat and help people who were really suffering. For the first time in a long time, I was happy. The *Boston Globe* ad had been beckoning me for weeks, but I had ignored it. Finally I noticed the coincidence and I was able to change my destiny. Even though laboratory work seemed to be the very thing I had been striving for all my life, paying attention to this coincidence allowed me to break my habitual patterns. It was a message just for me, my life's personal road flare. Everything I had done up to that point was simply preparation for that change. Some people thought the endocrinology fellowship itself was a mistake. But if I hadn't gotten the fellowship, I might not have been in Boston. And if I wasn't working in the endocrinologist's lab, I might not have seen that ad and I might never have felt my heart's true calling. Endless details had to fall into place in order for this part of my life to play out the way it has.

According to a poem by Rumi, one of my favorite poets and philosophers, "This is not the real reality. The real reality is behind the curtain. In truth, we are not here. This is our shadow." What we experience as everyday reality is merely a shadow play. Behind the curtain there is a soul, living and dynamic and immortal, beyond the reach of space and time. By acting from that level, we can consciously influence our destiny. This happens through the *synchronization* of seemingly *acausal* relationships to mold a *destiny*—hence, synchrodestiny. In synchrodestiny, we consciously participate in the creation of our lives by understanding the world that is beyond our senses, the world of the soul.

THE COINCIDENCE OF THE UNIVERSE

Nothing—absolutely nothing—would exist were it not for a remarkable set of coincidences. I once read an article by a physicist describing the Big Bang that gave birth to our universe. In that moment, the number of particles created was slightly more than the number of antiparticles. The particles and the antiparticles then collided and annihilated each other, filling the universe with photons. Because of the initial imbalance, there were a few particles left after the annihilation and these created what we know as the material world. You and I and the rest of the universe, including all the stars and galaxies, are leftover stuff from the moment of creation. The total number of particles left over was 10^{80} (that's the number 1 followed by 80 zeros). If the number of particles had been even slightly greater, gravitational forces would have forced the young universe to collapse on itself, forming one huge black hole, which would mean no you, no me, no stars, or galaxies. If the number of matter-particles had been even slightly smaller, the universe would have expanded so fast that there would have been no time for the galaxies to form as they did.

The first atoms were hydrogen. If the strong force that holds the nucleus of an atom were even a fraction percent weaker, deuterium, a stage that hydrogen passes through before becoming helium, would not have occurred and the universe would have remained pure hydrogen. If, on the other hand, the nuclear forces were even a fraction stronger, all the hydrogen would have burned rapidly, leaving no fuel for the stars. So just as the gravitational forces needed to be exactly the strength they were, the electromagnetic forces that held electrons in place needed to be exactly as they were—not a fraction more or a fraction less—for stars to evolve into supernovas and for heavy elements to develop.

The development of carbon and oxygen, essential for the creation of biological organisms, required many coincidences to occur and to continue to occur from the moment of the Big Bang. That you and I exist, and that the universe with its stars, galaxies, and planets exists, is a highly improbable event! A total coincidence! A miracle, tracking back to the birth of time.

If you could have looked out on the universe at any particular point in that time, you would not have seen the entire pattern that was developing.

When stars were forming, you could not have imagined planets, not to mention giraffes and spiders and birds and humans. When sperm met egg to create the human being that you are, no one could have imagined the remarkable tale of your life, the fantastic twists and turns of your past, the people you would meet, the children you would bear, the love you would create, the impression you would leave upon this earth. And yet here you are, living proof of daily miracles. Just because we cannot observe miracles the way we marvel over magic tricks—with instantaneous gratification—does not mean that they are not occurring. Many miracles take time to be revealed and appreciated.

Here's another example from my life, one that illustrates the slow mechanics of synchronicity. It started one day when I was about ten or eleven years old and my father took me and my brother to see a cricket match between India and the West Indies. The Caribbean countries had amazing cricketers, some of whom could hurl the ball 95 miles an hour. During that game, India was being walloped by the West Indies, down by five wickets for a few runs, which is a disaster in cricket. And then two young players came on the scene. To protect their privacy I'll call them Saleem and Mohan.

They were amazing. They civilized the game, defended every ball, and scored "sixers" at every turn. Because of them, the India team went on to win this absolutely impossible match. There were near-riots in the stadium from celebration. People burned the wickets. For my brother and me, these two cricketers became our heroes. All we did was dream of cricket. We created a cricket club, and we started a scrapbook to collect information about Mohan and Saleem.

Forty years later, three friends and I were traveling in Australia. We couldn't get a taxi to the airport because they were overwhelmed with business due to a cricket match going on between the Australia and West Indies teams. We couldn't even hire a car because they were all taken. Eventually, the hotel concierge told us that there was a limousine going to the airport—there were other people in it, but they didn't mind sharing. We felt lucky to find a ride and got in the limo. Inside were a woman named Kamla and another man. As we drove to the airport, every once in a while we would hear the driver of the limo screaming and we wondered what was going on. He told us that the West Indies was soundly beating the Australia cricket team. At that moment, my consciousness was totally flooded by memories of that childhood match. It was such an amazing feeling that I shared it with my fellow passengers. The match had taken place decades earlier, but I could still describe it in every detail.

When we finally got to the airport ticket counter, the clerk told Kamla that her flight wasn't scheduled until the following afternoon. She had come on the wrong day! She asked if she could get a flight that day, but no, they were all completely booked. She called her hotel to arrange another night's stay, but they, too, were full thanks to the cricket match. So we suggested that she come with us to Brisbane. One of my friends told Kamla about the conspiracy of improbabilities, how coincidences were clues to the will of the universe. She ended up joining us on our flight. On the plane, the Indian fellow sitting on my left recognized me and pulled out a copy of one of my books, *The Seven Spiritual Laws of Success*. He asked me if I would sign it. I asked his name, and he said, "Ramu." I said, "Okay, Ramu. What's your last name?" He said, "Menon." I said, "You're not Mohan Menon's son, are you?" He said he was. Mohan Menon was my hero decades ago at that cricket match with my brother! We ended up talking for two hours. I was totally overcome with emotion. For me, it was like talking with the son of Babe Ruth. I asked if he played cricket, and he said not now, but in his time he had played with some great cricketers. When I asked whom he played with, he said, "Ravi Mehra." As soon as he said that, Kamla, sitting behind me, squealed. Ravi Mehra was her brother. When they started talking, it turned out that they each had business contacts the other could use, and were later able to help each other in a way that brought both of them considerable wealth. And I was the lucky catalyst in transforming the lives of these two strangers whom I had just met! Some forty years after that first cricket match, the complex and unforeseeable web of relationships created fresh opportunities. You never know how and when any life experience will reappear. You never know when a coincidence will lead to the opportunity of a lifetime.

ATTENTION AND INTENTION

Consciousness orchestrates its activity in response to both attention and intention. Whatever you put your attention on becomes energized. Whatever you take your attention away from dwindles. On the other hand, intention is the key to transformation, as we have seen. So you could say that attention activates the energy field, and intention activates the information field, which causes transformation.

Every time you speak you transmit information through an energy field using sound waves. Every time you send or receive e-mail, you use both information and energy. There is information in the words you select, and the energy is the electromagnetic impulse that travels through cyberspace. Information and energy are inseparably connected.

Have you ever noticed how, when you start paying attention to a particular word or color or object, that very thing seems to appear more often in your environment? My first car was a Volkswagen Beetle. I never really paid much attention to cars, and I rarely noticed Volkswagens on the road. But after I bought my Beetle, I saw them everywhere. It seemed that every third car on the road was a red, convertible Beetle! It's not that these little cars were playing a bigger part in the universe, but my attention to them made anything associated with Beetles "pop" into my field of attention.

Millions of things happen every day that never penetrate our conscious minds: sounds from the street, conversations of people around us, newspaper articles that our eyes quickly scan, patterns on clothing, shoe colors, smells, textures, flavors. Our consciousness can handle only so much information, so we have selective attention. Whatever we choose to focus our attention on will make it past the mind's filtering system. For example, imagine that I'm talking to you at a party. You and I are having an interesting conversation and the rest of the party is buzzing in the background. But then somebody at the end of the room starts talking about you, and suddenly you start listening to what's being said. The buzz of the party disappears, and even though I might be standing right next to you talking in your ear, you don't hear me. Such is the power of attention.

In the physical world, we have many different

ways of acquiring information: newspapers, books, television, radio, cell phone conversations, shortwave radios—all these ways of tapping into various kinds of information, and many more, are readily available to us. You can simply tune in to them with your sensory apparatus—look, listen, feel, smell, taste the environment around you. But if you want to tap in to the information at the level of the soul, you need a different way to get the information.

We don't normally have our attention in that unseen dimension, but everything that's happening in the visible world has its roots there. Everything is connected with everything else. In the spiritual world, those connections become visible. But in the physical world, we only glimpse the connections in the clues given to us through coincidence. As our attention creates energy, intention brings about the transformation of that energy. Attention and intention are the most powerful tools of the spiritually adept. They are the triggers for attracting both a certain kind of energy and a certain kind of information.

So the more attention you put on coincidences, the more you attract other coincidences, which will help you clarify their meaning. Putting your attention on the coincidence attracts the energy, and then asking the question "What does it mean?" attracts the information. The answer might come as a certain insight, or intuitive feeling, or an encounter, or a new relationship. You may experience four seemingly unrelated coincidences, then watch the evening news and have an insight. Ah-ha! That's what they meant for me! The more attention you put on coincidences and the more you inquire into their significance, the more often the coincidences occur and the more clearly their meaning comes into view. Once you can see and interpret the coincidences, your path to fulfillment emerges.

In most people's experience, the past resides only in memory and the future resides only in imagination. But at the spiritual level, the past and the future and all the different probabilities of life exist simultaneously. Everything is happening all at once. It's as if I'm playing a CD, and the CD has twenty-five tracks, but at the moment, I'm listening to only track 1. Those other tracks are still on the CD at this very moment; I'm just not hearing them. And if I'm unaware of them, I may assume they don't exist. If I had a track changer for my life experience, I could listen to yesterday, today, or tomorrow with equal ease. People who are tuned in to the deeper self can access this deeper domain because this self is not separate from the universe; the Buddhists say that your "self" is an inter-being that is interlinked with all that exists. You are inseparably part of the cosmic quantum soup.

NURTURING COINCIDENCE

Now we know that putting your attention on coincidences attracts more coincidences, and applying intention reveals their meaning. In this way coincidences become clues to the will of the universe, providing a way for us to see its synchronicity and take advantage of life's boundless opportunities. But with billions of different pieces of information coming at us at any given time, how do we know what to put our attention on? How do you keep from looking for meaning in every cup of tea, or every television commercial, or every glance from a stranger on the street? And conversely, how do we keep from missing valuable opportunities?

Those questions cannot be answered simply. Part of learning to live synchrodestiny is learning to become a sensitive instrument in your surroundings. For a moment now, close your eyes. Try to sense everything in your environment. What sounds do you hear? What do you smell, feel, or taste at this very moment? Put your attention for a moment on each sense individually and be fully aware.

If you have not performed this exercise before, you will likely have missed some of these common stimuli—not because they are faint, but because we grow so accustomed to them that we no longer pay them any mind. For example, what did you *feel*? What was the temperature? Was there a breeze, or was the air still? What parts of your body were making contact with the chair you are sitting in? Did you notice the pressure on the backs of your thighs, or on your lower back? What about sounds? Most of us can easily pick out the distant barking of a dog, or the noise of children playing in the next room, but what about more subtle sounds? Could you hear the blowing of the furnace or air conditioner? Could you hear yourself breathing? Your stomach growling? What about the faint hum of traffic?

People who are sensitive to events and stimuli around them will be sensitive to coincidences sent from the universe. The clues we receive will not always come in the mail or flash on a television screen (although sometimes they will). Clues may be as subtle as the smell of pipe smoke wafting through an open window, which makes you think of your father, which reminds you of a book he loved, which then somehow comes to play an important role in your life at the moment.

At least once a day, focus for a minute or two on one of your five senses—sight, hearing, taste, touch, smell—and allow yourself to notice as many different aspects of this sense as possible. Although this will take effort initially, you'll soon find yourself doing it naturally. Close off other senses if you find them too distracting. For example, try eating different foods while holding your nose and closing your eyes; focus on the texture of the food, without being distracted by sight or smell.

The most powerful and unusual stimuli will naturally draw your attention. Those are the things in your environment you need to look at most closely. And the more unlikely the coincidence, the more potent the clue. If you are considering getting married, becoming more aware of advertisements for wedding rings is a minor coincidence because these advertisements are abundant. But having a banner reading JOANNA, MARRY ME fly over your head while you are considering proposing to Joanna is highly unlikely, and a very powerful message about the path the universe has planned for you.

When a coincidence arises, don't ignore it. Ask yourself, What is the message here? What is the significance of this? You don't need to go digging for the answers. Ask the question, and the answers will emerge. They may arrive as a sudden insight, a spontaneous creative experience, or they may be something very different. Perhaps you will meet a person who is somehow related to the coincidence that occurred. An encounter, a relationship, a chance meeting, a situation, a circumstance will immediately give you a clue to its meaning. "Oh, so that's what it was all about!"

Consider how my final-straw argument with the endocrinologist finally gave meaning to the *Boston Globe* want ad I had been noticing but not attending to. The key is to pay attention and inquire.

Another thing you can do to nurture coincidence is to keep a diary or journal of coincidences in your life. After years of note-taking, I classify coincidences as tiny, medium, whoppers, and double-whoppers. You can do this in any way that is easy for you. For some people, it is easiest to maintain a daily journal and underline or highlight words or phrases or names of things that show up as coincidences. Other people keep a special coincidence diary. They start a new page for each significant coincidence, then jot down any other connections to that event on its page.

For people who want to delve deeply into coincidence, one of the processes I recommend is recapitulation. This is a way of putting yourself in the position of observer of your life, and of your dreams, so that connections and themes and images and coincidences become clearer. Because our connection to the universal soul is much more obvious when we are dreaming, this process allows you to access a whole new level of coincidences.

When you go to bed at night, before you fall asleep, sit up for a few minutes and imagine that you are witnessing on the screen of your consciousness everything that happened during the day. See your day as a movie. Watch yourself waking up in the morning, brushing your teeth, having breakfast, driving to work, conducting

your business, coming home, eating dinner—
everything in your day right up to bedtime. There
is no need to analyze what you see, or evaluate, or
judge . . . just watch the movie. See it all. You may
even notice things that did not strike you as
important at the time. You may notice that the
color of the hair of the woman behind the drug-
store counter was the same as your mother's when
you were young. Or you might pay special attention to a little child who was crying as his mother
was dragging him down a supermarket aisle. It's
amazing the things that show up in the movie of
your day that you may not have consciously
noted during the day itself.

As you watch your day go by in the movie, take
this opportunity to view yourself objectively. You
may find yourself doing something that you're
particularly proud of, or at times you may notice
yourself doing things that are embarrassing.
Again, the goal is not to evaluate, but to get little
insights into the protagonist's behavior—this
character that is your self.

When the recapitulation is over—which can
take as little as five minutes or as long as a half
hour—say to yourself, "Everything that I've witnessed, this movie of a day in my life, is now safely
stored away. I can summon those images on the
screen of my consciousness but as soon as I let
them go, they disappear." The movie is over. Then,
as you go to sleep, say to yourself, "Just as I now
recapitulated the day, I am giving instructions to

my soul, my spirit, my subconscious to witness my dreams." Initially you may not notice much of a change. But if you practice this every night for a few weeks, you will start to have a very clear experience that the dream is the scenery, and you are the person watching it all. When you wake up in the morning, recapitulate the night, just as you recapitulated the day at night.

Once you are able to recall the movie of your dreams, write down some of the more memorable scenes. Include them in your journal. Make a special note of coincidences. Nonlocal intelligence provides clues in our sleep just as it does in our waking hours. During the day I meet people, I have interactions, I find myself in situations or circumstances, events, relationships . . . and in the night I also find myself in those situations. The difference is that in the day, there seems to be a logical, rational explanation for what happens. Our dreams are not only projections of our own consciousness; they are, in fact, how we interpret our life paths. The mechanics of the dream and the mechanics of what is happening to us in the so-called reality are the same projections of the soul. We are merely witnesses.

What starts to happen, then, is that gradually we see correlations, images that repeat themselves both in dreams and in everyday reality. More coincidences provide more clues to guide our behavior. We start to enjoy more opportunities. We have more "good luck." These clues point out the direction to take our lives. Through this process of recapitulation we see recurring patterns and we start to unravel life's mystery.

This process is especially helpful for departing from destructive habits. Life has certain themes that it plays out. Sometimes those themes operate to our advantage. Sometimes they work against us, especially if we repeat the same patterns or themes, over and over, hoping to get a different result. For example, many people who get divorced fall in love again, but they end up in exactly the same kind of relationship they were in before. They repeat the same trauma, relive the same anguish, and then they say, "Why does this keep happening to me?" The process of recapitulation can help us witness these patterns, and once we discern them, we can make more conscious choices. Journaling isn't absolutely necessary, but it helps bring insights and coincidences to the surface.

So remain sensitive, observe coincidences during both your daytime living and your nighttime dreaming, and pay special attention to anything that breaks the probability amplitude—the statistical likelihood of a space-time event. We all need to plan things to some extent, to make assumptions about tomorrow even though we actually don't know what's going to happen. Anything that upsets our plans, anything that takes us off the trajectory we think we are on, can provide a major insight. Even the absence of events that you expect can be clues to the intent of the universe. People who have a hard time getting out of bed in the morning to go to a job they hate, who find it difficult to become engaged in their professional activities, who feel emotionally "dead" after a day at the office, need to pay attention to those feelings. These are important signals that there must be a way to get more fulfillment out of life. Perhaps a miracle lies in the wings. You'll never know unless you form an intention, become sensitive to the clues from the universe, follow the chain of coincidence, and help create the destiny you most desire.

Of course, life can be difficult, and we each have daily chores, responsibilities, and obligations that can become overwhelming. Coincidences may come flying at you from all directions, or they may seem to dry up entirely. How do you find your way in such a complex world? Take five minutes every day and just sit in silence. In that time, put these questions to your attention and heart: "Who am I? What do I want for my life? What do I want from my life today?" Then let go, and let your stream of consciousness, your quieter inner voice, supply the answers. Then, after five minutes, write them down. Do this every day and you'll be surprised at how situations, circumstances, events, and people will orchestrate themselves around the answers. This is the beginning of synchrodestiny.

For some people, answering those questions for

the first time can be difficult. Many of us are not used to thinking in terms of our own wants and needs, and if we do, we certainly don't expect to fulfill them. If you haven't defined your life's goal for yourself, what do you do then? It would be helpful if the universe would give us one big clue, or a giant compass, if you will, pointing to the direction we should be taking. In fact, the compass is there. To find it, you need only look inside yourself to discover your soul's purest desire, its dream for your life. Sit quietly. Once you reveal this desire and understand its essential nature, then you have a constant beacon, which we can make manifest in the form of archetypal symbols.

Desires and Archetypes

W e come now to the heart of synchrodestiny. We have discovered the dual nature of the soul, and we understand that we are fully part of the nonlocal intelligence, just as a wave is part of the ocean. We have learned to see the synchronicity in all things, the matrix that links us to the source of the universe. We have learned to value coincidences as messages from the nonlocal intelligence that point us in the direction of our destiny, and we know that our intentions can influence this direction. All these revelations are essential for living a fulfilled life. But when we look for guidance in how to construct our everyday lives, we still need to answer the central question of self: What are my dreams and desires? And that can only be answered by asking, in addition, Who am I? What do I want? What's my purpose in this lifetime?

We know that our deepest relationships and meanings and contexts derive from the soul. And our aspiration, that grand and wonderful and mythical thing that we yearn to do, also ultimately derives from the soul. In our time here on earth, this individual soul will not be fulfilled unless it completes its mythical quest, which we can think of as the Grand Plan around which our destinies are organized. Inside every human being there is an overarching theme, a template for heroic living, a god or a goddess in embryo that yearns to be born. This is who we were meant to be, the self that we deny ourselves because most of us cannot see the field of limitless potential that is open to us. This is our best self, the egoless self, that bit of the universe acting through us for the good of all.

People who live ordinary, mundane lives have not gotten in touch with the mythical being inside them. You can pave the path to enlightenment by understanding the plan written on your soul, by nurturing the relationships that give you context and meanings, and by enacting your mythical drama. Out of that is born love and compassion. Out of that comes fulfillment and completion.

These mythical stories, these heroes and heroines within, are called archetypes. Archetypes are perennial themes that reside at the level of the collective, universal soul. These themes are representations of our collective soul's yearnings, imagination, and deepest desires. These themes have existed forever. We see them in the writings of ancient cultures, in literature throughout the ages. Their shapes shift depending on where we are in history, but their core remains the same. These archetypes are enacted in modern-day movies, television soap operas, and tabloid newspapers. Anytime a person or character is "bigger than life," we are seeing the enactment of an archetype. These characters are usually presented as uncomplicated, with purity of intent, regardless of what that intent may be. Divine or diabolical, sacred or profane, the sinner or the saint, the adventurer, the sage, the seeker, the rescuer, the love object, the redeemer—all are exaggerated expressions of the conscious energy of the collective soul.

Archetypes are born of the collective soul, but they are enacted by individual souls. Their mythical dramas play out daily in our physical world. We can look at Marilyn Monroe and easily see the embodiment of Aphrodite, a goddess of sex and beauty. We can see Robert Downey Jr. as the embodiment of Dionysus or Bacchus, the untamed, fun-loving spirit. Princess Diana was Artemis, the nonconformist, the wild one, the rule breaker, the fearless warrior who fights for what she believes.

Every human being is attuned to some archetype, or two or three archetypes. Every one of us is hardwired at the level of the soul to enact or model archetypal characteristics. They are seeds sown within us. When a seed sprouts, it releases the patterning forces that allow it to grow into a certain type of plant. A tomato seed will always grow to be a tomato plant, not a rosebush. The activation of an archetype releases its patterning forces that allow us to become more of what we already are destined to be. And our individual archetypes are reflected in our desires or intentions. So, who are you? What do you want? What is the purpose of your existence? At the deepest level these questions are asked of the soul. And to find the answers you must speak to that part of the soul that is unique to you. And as we do, we learn to define our individual archetypes.

We live in a society that is so totally goal oriented that everything has to have a label, but this is less helpful when you explore the nature of your soul. Some people call me an author. Others call me a spiritual thinker, or a mind-body doctor, or a personal adviser. My children think of me as a father, and my wife sees me as her mate. All these roles help to define me, but who I am is continually emerging as my destiny unfolds. If you label yourself, you become stuck, like a butterfly caught in a jar. Adopting an archetype is not labeling because it is not about limitations. Quite the opposite. Archetypes are life models, images and ideas that guide the direction of your life toward your soul's ultimate destiny. Recognizing your true nature and allowing it to blossom is part of the beauty of living from the level of the soul—you become the hero or heroine of a mythical saga.

If we allow ourselves to become swayed by forces in the physical world, whether they are well-meaning or not, then we are lured away from our soul's destiny. We start to desire things that may not be meant for us; we begin to have intentions that do not match up with the intentions of the universe. What do these forces look like? They can be as innocent as friends giving advice they think is in your best interest; they can be as pervasive as media messages enticing us to buy an endless line of products; they can be as seductive as a corner office with the title of corporate vice president and a seven-figure salary. These are messages from the physical world, not from the universe. The blueprint that the universe intends for you is found at the level of the soul. We get clues in the form of coincidences, and we get guidance in the form of archetypes.

So how do you know which destiny is meant for you, and which dream is just the product of our mass-market culture? How many little girls dream of being the next Britney Spears? How many little boys aspire to be the next Michael Jordan? We emulate these celebrities because they are enacting their own archetypes, they succeeded in following their own inner quests. You can begin to know your own archetypes and your own destiny only by accessing the will of the universal soul, by looking deep inside and defining your innermost desires, by choosing the archetype that most closely matches your intentions, and following its ancient pattern.

THE PURPOSE OF ARCHETYPES

Discovering archetypes is a highly personal experience. No one can look at you, even if they know you well, and tell you, "Oh, you are this archetype." Vedic science, the ancient wisdom tradition of India, says that unless you can get in touch with that embryo of a god or goddess incubating inside you, unless you can let that embryo be fully born, then your life will always be mundane. But once that god or goddess expresses itself through you, then you will do grand and wondrous things.

These days, we tend to seek symbolic archetypes in celebrities, but we need to nurture a full expression of the archetypes in ourselves. They are part of what creates us. This is the stuff our dreams are made of. This is the stuff of mythology, of campfire stories, of legends. This is what inspires great movies. In *Star Wars* Luke Skywalker is the expression of the archetype of the eternal adventurer, willing to take risks to explore the unknown. Princess Leia is like Artemis, the independent huntress, the protector. Yoda is the wise seer, the keeper of powerful knowledge who is connected to the nonlocal intelligence. These are figures of our collective imagination, ancient archetypes in futuristic form.

Archetypes are vital to understanding and defining who we are, individual expressions of a collective consciousness. Mythology is the wellspring of our civilization. One of the consequences of depriving people of mythology is that they join street gangs. Why? Because gangs have a leader, they have rituals, they have initiation rites—the stuff of mythology. Our children are joining gangs in search of a mythical experience. Whenever somebody does anything remarkable—when astronauts walk on the moon, when a pilot embarks on the first solo flight across the Atlantic—these are mythical quests, Jason in search of the Golden Fleece, Icarus soaring in his wings of feathers and wax. From Persephone's abduction by Pluto to Orpheus seeking his bride among the shades of Hades, to Apollo, Krishna, and all the stories of Celtic mythology—this is the deepest wellspring of civilization and identity.

Gangs and movies and soap operas and celebrities are seductive precisely because they strike this mythic chord. But they are second-class substitutes for mythology. Real archetypes are enacted by people like Mahatma Gandhi, Martin Luther King Jr., Rosa Parks, anyone who reaches beyond daily life into the realm of the wondrous. They are able to achieve greatness because they tapped into the collective consciousness, which gave them the ability to see several event lines simultaneously and predict the future based on choices in the moment. They say that when Mahatma Gandhi was thrown out of the train in Durban, South Africa, he closed his eyes and saw the British Empire crumbling halfway across the world. That one episode changed the course of history.

These events create a shift in cognitive and perceptual mechanisms. Normally this hardware allows us to see only what's happening here, right in front of us. But from time to time we can awaken dormant potentialities and the wisdom to use them. In Sanskrit, these are referred to as *siddhis*, which means supernormal powers—extrasensory perception, synchronicity, telepathy—all products of the nonlocal domain. These are the powers that bloom as myth.

FINDING YOUR ARCHETYPES

The process of finding an archetype should be joyous. Don't worry about choosing unwisely. Because archetypes spring from the collective consciousness, every archetype is present in every one of us. But some archetypes are represented more strongly. Your goal is to find the one, two, or even three archetypes that resonate with you most powerfully, those that represent your heart. Do not choose who you wish to be, or even which qualities you most admire, but seek out the qualities that you feel drawn to, that motivate you, that inspire you. You will know them when you find them. Best of all, there are no wrong answers.

To help you on your search, try the following exercise, which has been modified from the work of my friend Jean Houston, author of *A Mythic Life: Learning to Live Our Greater Story*. She has many other exercises in her books, which I highly recommend. Get comfortable and clear your mind. Ideally, the following paragraphs would be read to you while your eyes are closed; if possible record them on tape or CD and play them back so you can imagine the scenes more clearly. But reading with a clear and open mind can work, too.

Start by taking a few deep breaths. Slowly inhale and exhale, releasing any tension or tightness or resistance that you're carrying in your body. Keep taking slow, deep, smooth breaths, allowing each exhalation to take you to a deeper, quieter, and more relaxed place.

Now imagine that you are walking along a beautiful, tree-lined country path, far from the turbulence of the city. You observe the lush countryside as you stroll along, with birds soaring overhead, white-tailed rabbits scampering across the path, and butterflies fluttering about. You come to a clearing and you notice a charming, rustic cottage with a thatched roof. The door is open and welcoming. You look inside and see a den and a hallway leading to the back of the house. You feel very safe and comfortable here, as if you're returning to your own home, and you begin to walk down the hallway into a small room. You notice a closet door, which you open. Pushing aside the clothes, you discover an opening at the back of the closet. Moving through the opening, you find that it leads to an ancient stone staircase, which winds down and around, down and around. The light is dim, so you carefully descend, one step at a time, holding onto the railing and being very careful not to fall, descending deeper and deeper and deeper. You finally reach the bottom of the stairway and you find yourself at the edge of a broad river reflecting rays of silvery moonlight. Sitting by the side of the river, you listen to its hushed passage and gaze into the star-filled eternity of the night sky.

Off in the distance you see a small boat sailing toward you. It glides up, and a figure shrouded in linen robes stands in the boat and beckons you to enter. Feeling safe and protected, you step aboard and you're given a flowing garment, decorated with ancient symbols, to change into. The boat sails through a narrow tunnel, which seems to go on forever. The bearded boatman in the stern begins chanting some unfamiliar mantras, and after a few moments you notice that your senses have become much more alert. You're relaxed yet curiously exhilarated.

A light appears at the end of the tunnel and grows brighter. As you move closer to the light, you become aware that it is an invitation to enter the virtual realm. As you accept, and immerse yourself in the light, you suddenly find yourself becoming weightless. You begin floating off the boat and experience yourself merging with this nourishing light. You become this light. You are now a virtual being, a sphere of pulsating light. From this realm of pure potentiality, you can emerge into quantum and material reality in any form or shape, and at any location in space-time that you choose.

You reach into the depths of your light being and emerge as the goddess Hera, Queen of Olympus and all the gods of Greece, the symbol of regal power and beauty. You're in command of the world, filled with confidence and authority. Your subjects rely upon your certainty and strength. You are the ultimate expression of self-assurance. Feel what it is like to have the consciousness of this powerful goddess. Feel the sensations of moving in her body. Feel what it is like to have her gestures, to have her speech, her facial expressions. Look at the world through her eyes. Hear the world through her ears.

Now bid farewell to this goddess and return to your virtual light form. Once again you're in the realm of pure potential, pulsating with possibilities. Reach into the depths of your light being and emerge as the wise old king, skilled in the ways of navigating the storms of life. You are the bearded sage, the great *rishi* who sees the forms and phenomena of the world as a cosmic dance. You are in this world but not of it, and each of your thoughts, words, and actions expresses absolute impeccability. Feel what it is like to have the consciousness of a sage. Your mind is the mind of a seer. Feel what it is like to have his thoughts, his speech, and his gestures. See the world through his eyes.

Now release the seer and again merge back into your essence as a virtual light being. Reach into your depths and emerge as the redeemer. You are the light of compassion, radiant with forgiveness and hope. Your very presence dispels the darkness, no matter how foreboding it may seem. You are the essence of avatars, the essence of Christ, of Buddha. Your very nature transforms experience into faith. Witness the thoughts that arise in the mind of the redeemer. Feel the emotions in the heart of the redeemer. Experience the world through the eyes of the redeemer, overflowing with compassion and love for all sentient beings.

Now release the redeemer and return to your primordial essence. You are a virtual light being, a distilled pool of universal energy. You are the full potential of all that was, is, and will be. Reach into the depths of this light nature and emerge as the divine mother. You are the essential nurturing force, alive with life-giving energy. You are Demeter, Shakti, the feminine face of God. You are the divine mother, bestowing your loving kindness on all sentient beings. You are the primordial creative force, giving birth to forms and phenomena. Experience the consciousness of the divine mother. Feel the feelings of the divine mother. See creation through her eyes. Hear creation through her ears. Inhale and exhale the breath of the divine mother.

Now release the divine mother. Resume your essential nature as pure light, the primordial virtual energy, alive with possibilities to manifest anything you choose to become. Plunge into the depths of your being and emerge as Dionysus, the god of sensuality, of ecstasy and intoxication, the god of excess and abandon. You are the personification of total surrender into the moment. Your nature is to hold nothing back, to immerse yourself in the experience of being alive. You are drunk with love. Experience the world with the consciousness of Dionysus. Feel intoxication. Perceive the world through Dionysian eyes. Hear the music of the universe as a celebration of your being. Give yourself over to the ecstasy of the senses and of the spirit.

Now release Dionysus and merge back into your primordial energy state of pure virtual light.

Find the impulse of wisdom and intelligence within your infinite potential and emerge as the goddess of wisdom, Saraswati or Athena. You're the protector of civilization with your commitment to knowledge, wisdom, the arts, and scientific knowledge. You're a true spiritual warrior, dedicated to destroying any ignorance that impedes the expression of truth. Experience the consciousness of a goddess of wisdom. Look at the world through her eyes; hear the prevailing conversation through her ears. You are refinement, you are elegance, and you are civility and wisdom at its highest value.

And now let go of the goddess of wisdom. Return to your original state of pure virtual light. Merge back into your unbounded, unmanifest being, pulsing with potential. Dive into your essential light essence and emerge as Aphrodite, as Venus, the goddess of love and beauty. You're the embodiment of sensuality, passion, and sexuality. In your presence, sentient beings lose their heads and crave the rapture of Eros. Express and experience the consciousness of the goddess of love. Experience the body of the goddess of sensuality. Savor her sensuality. See the world through the eyes of the goddess of love.

Now release the love goddess, returning into your core as light, as pure undifferentiated being, as infinite possibilities. Dive deeply into your essence and emerge as the holy child, the expression of pure divine potential. You are the incarnation of innocence embodying the expectation of unconditional love, both as giver and as receiver. You are born of divine parents, and you are ripe with destiny and cosmic potential. Observe the world through the eyes of the holy child. Feel the love flowing through your heart of innocence. Experience your playfulness as a child of light, rejoicing in your own being.

Release the holy child. Experience yourself as a virtual light being. Rest in your boundlessness. You're a throbbing heartbeat of energy, capable of creating anything you desire. Dive deeply into your light core and emerge as the cosmic alchemist. You're the ultimate magician, capable of turning nothing into something and something into nothingness. You know the world of the senses to be nonsensical. You experience the material world as an expression of your conscious energy, which you can transform into matter with your intention and attention. You can assume any form you choose, living or inanimate, because you are consciousness in all its disguises. You are Krishna; you are infinite possibilities. Experience yourself as Krishna, the cosmic alchemist, capable of manifesting anything you choose. Experience yourself transmuting your thoughts into phenomena. See the universe through the eyes of Krishna. Experience the cosmos as your body. You are not in the universe; the universe is in you.

Now for the next few minutes, play with your creative energy, manifesting yourself as any form you choose. It may be one of the common archetypes we have just reviewed, or it may not. Become any being you would like to experience. Assume the consciousness of a great artist or musician. Experience the world as a powerful political leader. Become an eagle; experience the world as a soaring bird. Become a whale and experience the consciousness of a playful underwater being. There are no limits to your possible expressions. Enjoy your virtual self, exuberant with the knowledge and experience of your infinite potential. In this form you are all the many gods and goddesses, archetypes, and mythical images in one body. For the next few moments, allow any images, any phrases, any symbols, any words that arise to take shape in your consciousness.

When you feel that you have experienced a wide range of interesting possibilities, choose three archetypal images or symbols or words or phrases that resonate within you, that inspire and motivate you. They could be familiar gods or goddesses known to you, images, animals, symbols of the elements, forces of the cosmos, words, phrases, or any other quality that means something to you, anything that feels most comfortable when you experienced it in your mind. You should feel that if these people or qualities could come into your world and express themselves through you, you would be capable of grand and wondrous things. I always recommend that men choose at least one female or feminine archetype, and that women choose at least one male or masculine archetype. We all have both masculine and feminine qualities inside us, and to ignore one particular side of our selves is to smother that source of personal passion.

Write down your three symbols or archetypes. Then, begin to collect artwork or pictures or symbols or jewelry that remind you of this archetype. Some people create a small altar for their archetypes as a place to center the search for self. If the principal qualities of your archetypes can be expressed in words or phrases, write them on a piece of paper so that you have something to remind you of them. At least once a day, preferably after meditation, look at these reminders and silently issue them an invitation: "Please come and express yourself through me." Let them be a reminder of your life's inspiration. When you feel lost or distracted in the world, they will be your compass back to your true self.

Instead of following the latest fashion trend or emulating a movie star, model yourself, your thoughts, and your actions on your archetypes. People do this every day, without even realizing what it is they are doing. Have you ever heard the question "What would Jesus do?" Christians who feel stuck at a crossroads in their lives or who have to make a decision about how to act are encouraged to ask themselves that question. It is a way of using the powerful archetype of the redeemer, as embodied by Jesus Christ, as a life guide. Use your personal archetypes in the same way. Ask yourself, "Am I acting in a way that would be consistent with my archetypes?" This is a profound way of asking, "Am I being true to myself?" You will find fulfillment through your archetypes by allowing the gods/goddesses/totems/personalities to enact their drama through you. They are the keys to your true and miraculous destiny.

part two

PAVING
DESTINY'S
PATH

Meditation and Mantras

7

The most powerful tool we have for learning to live synchrodestiny, to see the connective patterns of the universe, to make miracles out of our desires, is meditation. Meditation allows us to place our attention and intention in these more subtle planes, giving us access to all that unseen, untapped information and energy.

If your doctor gave you a prescription to walk for twenty minutes twice a day, and told you that those walks alone would lead to good health, peace of mind, freedom from worry, increased success in your personal and professional life, would you follow her recommendation? Most people would at least give it a try. The synchrodestiny prescription is to meditate for fifteen to twenty minutes twice a day, followed by a moment of extending an invitation to your archetypes (as described in the previous chapter). If you do that twice a day, you'll start to see a transformation in your life. Beyond that, conduct yourself just as you always have before. Meditate in the morning, live the rest of your day, and then meditate again in the evening. That alone will start you on the road to transforming your life and creating the miracles you want.

Everything that you have read in this book has been preparation for the actual practice of meditation that will lead you to enlightenment and living synchrodestiny. That background isn't necessary; it's just fun. If everyone needed to understand quantum physics to get enlightened, then only quantum physicists would attain enlightenment. As it happens, the great pioneers of quantum physics also advanced the cause of spirit by questioning the deeper meaning of life. Some of these remarkable scientists include Wolfgang Pauli, who along with Carl Jung first spoke about synchronicity. Erwin Schrödinger, Paul Dirac, Werner Heisenberg, Max Planck, David Bohm, and John Wheeler are others who felt that quantum physics could never be understood unless we included consciousness as a primary component of fundamental reality. But you don't need to understand religion, or philosophy, or science to access spirit. All you need to do is pay attention to the following instructions.

Meditation is a simple process that is difficult to describe, but is very easy to do once you begin to practice it regularly. Here I will present the basics of meditation so that you can successfully apply the principles of synchrodestiny described in the rest of the book.

HOW TO MEDITATE

Our minds are constantly active, always jumping from thought to thought, emotion to emotion. Getting in touch with the nonlocal intelligence, the universal soul that lies within us and is part of us all, requires finding a way past the fog of distracting thoughts that typically hide it from us. We cannot fight our way through that barrier any more than we can fight our way through a real fog. If you want to see across the street on a foggy day, nothing you can do physically will help. You must wait, patiently and calmly, for the fog to thin and lift on its own. Once in a while, a clear patch will emerge, and you can glimpse what lies ahead. The same is true of thoughts. If we are quiet, we encounter moments of pure silence—I call them thought "gaps"—and through these gaps we can glimpse the deeper level of the soul. Each glimpse increases our understanding, and eventually our consciousness becomes expanded.

The purpose of meditation is to stop thinking for a time, wait for the fog of thought to thin, and glimpse the spirit within. Controlling the flood of thoughts is very difficult for most people. Beginners can sometimes become very frustrated, but frustration is just another thought, another emotion that gets in the way. The goal is to release all thoughts, quietly, passively.

A common way to begin meditation is to gently focus on one thing so that it becomes more difficult for stray thoughts to enter your mind. I like to start with a breathing meditation.

To begin meditation, find a comfortable position. Sit in a comfortable chair, with your feet flat on the ground. Place your hands in your lap with the palms facing upward. Close your eyes and begin witnessing your breath. Observe the inflow and outflow of your breath without attempting to control it in any way. You may find that your breathing spontaneously gets faster or slower, deeper or shallower, and may even pause for a time. Observe the changes without resistance or anticipation. Whenever your attention drifts away from your breath to a sound in the environment, or a sensation in your body, or a thought in your mind, gently return your awareness to your breathing.

This is the basic meditation. Once a person becomes comfortable with simply sitting quietly and focusing on breathing, I recommend adding a mantra, which creates a mental environment that will allow you to expand your consciousness.

MANTRAS

The word *mantra* has two components to it: *man*, which is the root sound of the word *mind*, and *tra*, which is the root sound of the word *instrument*. So, the word *mantra* literally means an instrument of the mind. The ancient wisdom tradition of Vedanta examined the various sounds produced in nature, the fundamental vibrations of the world around us. According to Vedanta, these sounds are an expression of the infinite or cosmic mind, and provide the basis for every human language. For example, if you sound out all the letters of the alphabet, the vowels and the consonants, you'll hear that these are the same sounds that all babies make spontaneously. These sounds also contain the same vibrations that animals make. And if you listen carefully, you'll notice that these sounds are everywhere in nature. These are the sounds of the wind, of fire crackling, of thunder, of the river rushing by, of ocean waves crashing on the shore. Nature is vibration. The infinite being vibrates, and that vibration is rhythmic, musical, and primordial. Vibration is the means through which infinite potential expresses itself as the manifest universe.

We know that the manifest universe—which appears to be made up of solid objects—is actually made up of vibrations, with different objects vibrating at different frequencies. Of course, if I kick a large rock, I don't feel vibration. I feel pain. But the fact is that the foot that feels the pain and the brain that records the pain are also vibration. Vibration interacts with vibration, and we interpret that as matter and sensation. *Mantra* is just a word that describes this quality of the universe.

The ancient seers are said to have heard these vibrations of the universe when they were in deep meditation. We can all hear these same vibrations any time. It is very simple. If you quiet your mind and sit silently, you will hear vibrations. You can try it any time you want. Even when you cover your ears, you'll hear them. Your body is also constantly vibrating, but the sounds are so subtle that you usually don't hear them. But if you sit quietly when there is no noise around you, you'll hear a background hum in the air. And if you start paying attention to that background hum, with practice you'll actually end up hearing all the mantras that have been recorded in the Vedic literature.

The Vedas also maintain that if you recite a mantra out loud, its special pattern of vibrations creates its own effects, and can create events in our current physical realm. Reciting the mantra mentally creates a mental vibration, which then becomes more abstract. Ultimately it takes you into the field of pure consciousness or spirit from where the vibration arose. So a mantra is a very good way to transcend and go back to the source of thought, which is pure consciousness. This is why specific mantras are recommended—because of the specific vibrations they induce.

The mantra I use, and that I recommend for achieving synchrodestiny, is the simple mantra "so-hum." This is the mantra of the breath; if you observe your breathing you'll hear "so-hum" as air moves in and out of your lungs. As you inhale, the sound of that vibration is "so." And as you exhale, the sound becomes "hum." If you want, you can experiment with this. Inhale deeply, close your eyes and your mouth, and exhale forcefully through your nose. If you concentrate, you'll hear the "hum" sound quite clearly.

One of the techniques of meditation is, in fact, simply focusing on where your breath comes from. With your eyes closed, inhale and think the word "so"; on the exhale, think the word "hum." Gradually both the breath and the sound will become quieter and quieter and quieter, and the breath becomes so quiet that it almost seems to stop. By quieting your breath, you quiet your mind. When you transcend, the mantra "so-hum" entirely disappears, and your breath pauses momentarily. Time itself comes to a stop and you're in the field of pure consciousness, the non-local domain, spirit, the ground of being.

The mantra, then, is a way to experience non-local consciousness. Aborigines, Indians, Native Americans, and many other traditional cultures have used it for thousands of years. In every tradition mantras involve chanting to create special vibrations, sounds of the universe that create something from nothingness, that move energy from the unmanifest into the manifest.

SUTRA

The sutra is a mantra that has meaning. The mantra itself has no meaning. It's just a vibration, a sound. It becomes a sutra when there's an intention coded in the sound. The word *sutra* is a Sanskrit word, related to the Latin noun *sutura*, which is the base of the English word *suture*, meaning "to join together by sewing." So a *sutra* is actually a stitch on the soul, and the stitch is one of intention. Both mantras and sutras allow you to transcend to a deeper consciousness. Therefore you could use the "so-hum" mantra, for example, to transcend. Then you could use an actual word, a sutra, to embed a particular intention into your consciousness.

The messages in a sutra are simple and complex at the same time. If I say the sutra *"aham brahmasmi"* ("the core of my being is the ultimate reality, the root and ground of the universe, the source of all that exists"), it might take a whole day, or half a book, to explain and understand that one sentence. Yet the sutra contains the complete understanding of that complex thought. So this sutra, these two words, summarizes the whole understanding. By simply putting your attention on this sutra, you will experience and understand the entire explanation contained within it.

There are mantras and sutras that have been used successfully for thousands of years, and you will find them in the chapters that follow. They provide a path to synchrodestiny. Although the Sanskrit words that embody those sutras may sound foreign to you, that doesn't diminish their effectiveness. You do not even have to understand the meanings of the sutras in order for them to work. Remember, these are the sounds of nature, with meaning attached. The soul will understand their meaning even if you do not.

Why do we use these ancient words as our mantras and sutras instead of more modern language? The answer has to do with potency. Using newer mantras and sutras only makes the process of experiencing synchronicity more difficult. Consider that there are many ways for me to go from my home to my office. I can take the highway. I can follow a road map or a contour map. I can take a helicopter. I can go to the coast and take a ship. But if I take a path that's well trodden, one that is familiar and that I've taken many times, then the journey is easier. Similarly, mantras and sutras that have been used for thousands of years by millions of people over generations provide the easiest route to transcendence and to the non-local domain.

But there's an additional value in using something that's been used many times before for a particular purpose. Every time a mantra or sutra is used, it helps increase the probability that a similar outcome will result from a later usage of the same mantra or sutra. If you recall the discussion of the wave-particle in Chapter 1, you'll remember that every time a wave-particle collapses as a particular wave pattern, it increases the likelihood that it will collapse as that same pattern of wave again in the future. Sutras are actually intentions that increase the statistical likelihood of the collapse of a wave function along predictable probability amplitudes. This means that the more a sutra is used, the greater the likelihood that its chosen intention will be fulfilled. Therefore it is better to use an old, well-used sutra than a new sutra. Try not to be put off by the use of Sanskrit, but welcome the ancient words as allies in your search for the transcendence that leads to synchrodestiny.

*T*he following chapters describe the seven Principles of Synchrodestiny and provide exercises to strengthen your understanding of them. These seven principles are ways of thinking about the qualities of nonlocal intelligence and relating them to your life. Each principle offers a new lesson, a new way of relating that brings you closer to spirit, with its infinite possibilities.

Here is the program for achieving synchrodestiny, a specific way to use all the elements I've discussed so far:

1. *Begin each day by going to a quiet place where you will not be disturbed. Gather symbols of your archetypes and place them in front of you.*

2. *Meditate for twenty minutes using the so-hum mantra. This expands your consciousness and puts you in a receptive frame of mind.*

3. *Immediately upon completing the meditation, when you open your eyes, look upon the symbols of your archetypes and invite or invoke the archetypal energies to express themselves through you. Say, "I ask that you become part of me and work through me. Guide me through my life."*

4. *Read the synchrodestiny principle for this day. There are seven Principles of Synchrodestiny and seven days of the week. On the day you begin, read the first principle. You don't have to understand every concept contained in that principle. Just read it. On the second day, move on to the second principle. On the third day, move on to the third principle, and so on. I recommend that you don't skip around; the principles are arranged in an order that builds, one upon the*

other. On the eighth day, go back to the first principle and start the series over again.

Each principle has a sutra that encapsulates the teachings of the principle. Thoroughly understand the meaning of the sutra. Perform the exercises associated with the sutra until they have become part of your reality. After many weeks, you will be able to read the sutra alone and gain the benefit of the entire chapter. Ideally, you will continue this program every day, with each week, each month bringing you closer to fulfilling your life's destiny.

These first four steps should take no longer than twenty or thirty minutes. Repeat the process at night.

For the rest of the day, you do not need to do anything special. Just live your life the way you normally would. The morning meditation focuses your intention for the day, even when you are not even thinking about it. By reading the principle, you create that intention, and then allow nonlocal intelligence to synchronize all the millions of individual events that need to occur to have the intention be fulfilled. That's all you need to do.

Although intention works on its own through synchronicity organized by nonlocal intelligence, synchronicity can become blocked by the ego. How can you tell when your ego is getting in the way of your dreams? There are many clues, but the most important is anxiety. Whenever your self or your spirit is overshadowed by your self-image or your ego, you feel anxiety. Your true, core self does not feel stress or anxiety. A person who is centered does not feel stress or anxiety. These feelings are a signal that your intimate connection to the nonlocal entity is blocked. For many people, this happens all too often. The way to break through this obstacle, and to regain the focus you lost by feeling stressed, or anxious, is through a process I call heliotropism.

Heliotropism is the natural mechanism in plants that allows them to always grow in the direction of light. By extension, I believe that your thoughts, your intentions, are the equivalent of that light, and the world itself grows in a direction to meet those intentions. Use the Sutra Statements at the end of each of the following seven chapters whenever you feel stressed, anxious, or lose your center during the day. Each day, simply turn to the Sutra Statement for that day. (You might find it helpful to photocopy these statements and carry them with you so you can use them when needed to reestablish your sense of self.) Read the first statement silently and allow an image to come to your consciousness. As soon as you register the image, say the sutra for that day (as included in the exercises). Do the same for each of that day's statements. As soon as you finish all the statements, which will take only about a minute or so, you should feel centered once again.

At the end of each chapter you will find one or more exercises designed to help illustrate the principles and guide you to a deeper understanding of the sutras. These are not part of the daily meditation, but a supplement. Try them whenever you feel you would like to take that extra step toward understanding the Principles of Synchrodestiny.

In the end, that's really all you need in order to reach the place where synchrodestiny happens— the seven principles, the seven sutras, your archetypes, an ability to meditate using the "so-hum" mantra, and the Sutra Statements to read when you feel yourself beginning to lose your center. In your hands these are the tools that make miracles happen.

8

The First Principle:
You Are a Ripple in the
Fabric of the Cosmos

SUTRA: Aham Brahmasmi *(ah-HUM brah-MAHS-mee)*

The core of my being is the ultimate reality, the root and ground of the universe, the source of all that exists.

The first principle of synchrodestiny acknowledges the underlying intelligence that gives rise to my body, your body, and the universe as a whole—everything from stars and galaxies to subatomic particles. This conscious intelligence field is the wellspring of the cosmos. It is the extended body we all share; it connects us all. The core of my being is also the core of your being, and the core of all beings.

You and I and the universe are the same. I am

the universe, localized in a single human being. You are also the universe, localized in your body, reading these words at this particular moment in space-time. We both exist only as particular ripples in the conscious intelligence field. Every aspect of ourselves is articulated and orchestrated by this boundless nonlocal intelligence, the endless sea of consciousness from which you and I and the universe arise. Even our thoughts, our wishes, our desires, our dreams are not technically *our* thoughts, wishes, desires, or dreams. They are manifestations of the total universe. And when you realize that the intentions and desires that arise in you are the very intentions of the universe, you can relinquish your desire for control and let the miraculous life you were born to lead unfold in all its unimaginable magnificence.

Once you understand this premise, you will understand the sutra of the first principle of synchrodestiny: The core of my being is the ultimate reality, the root and ground of the universe, the source of all that exists. As simple as this sounds, its depth can take a lifetime to plumb, and its meaning for our lives is profound. When we fully understand this simple sutra, everything becomes possible because everything already exists within us. You and I are the same, and each of us is the infinite being projecting a particular point of view—your point of view and my point of view. My self is inseparable from all that exists, just as your self is inseparable from all that exists.

The power in this thought emerges when we realize that the self functions synchronistically. Because I am an extension of the conscious intelligence, and the conscious intelligence is the source of all reality, then I am the source of all reality. I create my own experience.

*I*ntention springs from our deepest desires, and those desires are shaped by karma. You and I don't have the same karma; therefore we don't have exactly the same desires. We have loved different people, knelt at different graves, prayed at different altars. The specifics of desire are unique to each of us.

Yet if you follow the chain of desire, in the end we are all the same. We want to be happy. We want to be fulfilled. We want meaning and purpose in our lives. We want a sense of connection with God or spirit. We want other people to respect us and love us. And we want to feel safe. These desires are universal. But the route each of us takes to satisfy them is uniquely our own, based on our individual experiences and memories, or karma. We're all heading for the same destination, but we take different roads. We arrive together, having traveled our different paths.

Exercise 1:

THE SILENT WITNESS

Go to a quiet place where you are not likely to be disturbed. Put on a tape or CD of your favorite soothing music. Close your eyes. As you do so, turn your attention to who is really listening. Begin to notice two different facets of yourself. Your ears pick up the sound and your brain processes the notes, but that's only the mechanics of hearing. Who connects the notes so that they form music? As you are *thinking* about listening, who is doing the actual listening?

Notice the silent witness, the silent listener who is always present. This presence exists not only in yourself, but also in the space around you. It is that part of yourself that is beyond the thoughts and feelings of the moment, the part that never tires and never sleeps. Nor can this part of you ever be destroyed. Recognize that this silent witness is always there. It is that part of you that can be glimpsed when the chatter of your thoughts is silenced by meditation. Can you feel this deeper current of consciousness within you?

Awareness of this silent witness is the beginning of awareness of the conscious intelligence field—the source of all the synchronicities in our lives.

Exercise 2:

WHY ARE YOU HERE?

For this exercise you will need paper and pen, and ten minutes of uninterrupted time.

Ask yourself, Why am I here? Write down the first thing that comes to mind. This question is open to many interpretations, so jot down whatever thoughts it triggers. Don't worry about the writing itself. You don't even have to use complete sentences.

Then pose the question again: Why am I here? Write down a new response. Do this twenty times. Keep looking for different ways to interpret the question so that each answer is unique and speaks to a different facet of the question.

Now look over your responses. What do they tell you? Do you see any pattern or progression in the answers? What does this tell you about how you see your life?

You can see your life as a series of external and internal events, but you can also learn to see those events as connected with each other and with something more spiritual. When you do that, you will begin to see your life as an opportunity to share the special gift you alone can bestow upon the world. That's one answer to the question of why you are here. Having this kind of clarity of purpose will help you focus your intentions.

Sutra Statements
for the First Principle

Imagine that the whole universe is being played
out inside you.

(When you have an image in your mind,
say, "aham brahmasmi.")

Imagine that you are connected to everything
that exists.

(aham brahmasmi)

Imagine that you are like a crystal bead. You
reflect the light of all other sentient beings. You
also reflect the light of the whole universe.

(aham brahmasmi)

Imagine that you're a strand in the cosmic thread
connected to all the other strands.

(aham brahmasmi)

Imagine that you are eternal.

(aham brahmasmi)

9

The Second Principle: Through the Mirror of Relationships I Discover My Nonlocal Self

SUTRA: Tat Tvam Asi *(taht t'vahm AH-see)*

I see the other in myself and myself in others.

Understanding how human relationships work is one of the most important keys to synchrodestiny. In the West, we tend to rely on popular psychology to come up with strategies for managing our thoughts and feelings. All too often self-help books propose manipulating our relationships so they can become more satisfying. But creating positive human relationships is much more than a tactic: It means providing the human environment in which synchrodestiny can take place. It's absolutely fundamental, in the same way that gravity, or having air to breathe, is fundamental.

The mantra for this principle means "I am that." This principle builds on the first principle, in which we learned that we are all extensions of the universal energy field, all a single entity with different points of view. *I am that* involves looking at everything in the world, everyone else in the world, and realizing that you are looking at another version of yourself. You and I are the same. Everything is the same. I am that, you are that, all this is that. We are all mirrors for others, and we need to learn to see ourselves in the reflection of other people. This is called the mirror of relationship. Through the mirror of relationship I discover my nonlocal self. For this reason, nurturing relationships is the most important activity in my life. When I look around me, everything I see is an expression of myself.

Relationship, then, is a tool for spiritual evolution, with the ultimate goal of reaching unity consciousness. We are all inevitably part of the same universal consciousness, but the real breakthroughs happen when we start to recognize that connection in our daily lives.

Relationship is one of the most effective ways to access unity consciousness because we're always in relationships. Think of the web of relationships you have at any time—parents, children, friends, co-workers, romantic relationships. All are, at their heart, spiritual experiences. When you're in love, for example, romantically and deeply in love, you have a sense of timelessness. You are, at that moment, at peace with uncertainty. You feel wonderful but vulnerable, you feel intimate but exposed. You're transforming, changing, but without trepidation; you feel a sense of wonder. This is a spiritual experience.

Through the mirror of relationship—all relationships—we discover extended states of awareness. Those whom we love and those whom we are repelled by are both mirrors of ourselves. Whom are we attracted to? People who have the same traits as we have, but more so. We want to be in their company because subconsciously we feel that by doing so we, too, might manifest more of those traits as well. By the same token we are repelled by people who reflect back to us traits that we deny in our own selves. So if you are having a strong negative reaction to someone, you can be sure that they possess some traits in common with you, traits that you are not willing to embrace. If you were willing to accept those qualities, then they wouldn't upset you.

By recognizing that we can see ourselves in others, every relationship becomes a tool for the evolution of our consciousness. And as consciousness evolves, we experience expanded states of awareness. It is in those expanded states of awareness, when we get to the nonlocal domain, that we can experience synchrodestiny.

The next time you're attracted to someone, ask

yourself what attracted you. Is it beauty, or grace, or elegance, or influence, or power, or intelligence? Whatever it is, know that that quality is also blossoming in you. Pay attention to these feelings, and you can begin the process of becoming more fully yourself.

Of course, the same is true of people who repel you. In becoming more fully your true self, you have to understand and embrace the less attractive qualities in yourself. The essential nature of the universe is the coexistence of opposite values. You cannot be brave if you do not have a coward inside you. You cannot be generous if you do not have a tight-fisted person inside you. You cannot be virtuous unless you also contain the capacity for evil.

We spend much of our lives denying that we have this dark side to ourselves, and then end up projecting those dark qualities onto other people in our lives. Have you ever known people who naturally attract the "wrong" people into their lives? Usually they don't understand why this happens time after time, year after year. The truth is not that they attract that darkness, but that they are not willing to acknowledge it in their own lives. Finding a person you dislike is an opportunity to embrace the paradox of the coexistence of opposites, and to discover a new facet of yourself. It is another step toward developing your spiritual self. The most enlightened people in the world embrace their full potential of light and dark.

When you're with people who recognize and own their negative qualities, you never feel judged by them. It's only when people see good and bad, right and wrong, as qualities outside themselves that judgments occur.

When we are willing to embrace both the light and the dark sides of our selves, we can begin to heal both our selves and our relationships. Start very simply, with the most distasteful person you can think of. For example, think of Adolf Hitler and say, How could I possibly be like Hitler? Most people refuse to accept that they contain even the smallest shred of an Adolf Hitler. But think more deeply. Have you ever expressed prejudice toward any group of people just because they had a certain name, or a certain skin color, or a certain accent, or a certain disability? If you can think of any example of that in your life, then you must embrace the similarity between yourself and Adolf Hitler. We are all multidimensional, omni-dimensional. Everything that exists somewhere in the world also exists in us. When we embrace these different aspects of ourselves, we acknowl-edge our connection to the universal conscious-ness and expand our personal awareness.

There's a wonderful Sufi story that illustrates how this mirror affects our lives. A man entered a village and went to see the Sufi master, the wise old man of the village. The visitor said, "I'm decid-ing whether I should move here or not. I'm won-dering what kind of a neighborhood this is. Can you tell me about the people here?" The Sufi master said, "Tell me what kind of people lived where you came from." The visitor said, "Oh, they were highway robbers, cheats, and liars." The old Sufi master said, "You know, those are exactly the same kinds of people who live here." The visitor left the village and never came back. Half an hour later, another man entered the village. He sought out the Sufi master and said, "I'm thinking of moving here. Can you tell me what kind of people live here?" Again the Sufi master said, "Tell me what kind of people lived where you came from." The visitor said, "Oh, they were the kindest, gentlest, most compassionate, loving people. I shall miss them terribly." The Sufi master said, "Those are exactly the kinds of people who live here, too."

This story reminds us that the traits we see most clearly in others exist most strongly in our selves. When we can see into the mirror of relationship, then we can begin to see all of our selves. To do this, we need to be comfortable with our ambiguity, to embrace all aspects of our selves. At a deep level we need to recognize that we are not flawed simply because we have negative traits. No one has only positive traits. Recognizing that we have negative traits simply means that we are complete. And in that completeness we gain greater access to our universal, nonlocal selves.

Exercise 3:

EMBRACING DUALITY

For this exercise, you'll need a piece of paper and a pen.

Think about a specific person whom you find very attractive. On the left side of the paper list ten or more desirable qualities that person possesses. List anything that comes to mind. Write quickly. The secret is not to allow your conscious mind time to edit your thoughts. Why do you like this person? Why do you find him or her attractive? What do you most admire? Is that person kind, loving, flexible, independent? Do you admire that he or she drives a nice car, has a flattering hairstyle, or lives in a desirable house? You are the only one who will see this list, so be completely honest. If you get stuck before coming up with ten characteristics, then say out loud, "I like this person because _____," and fill in the blank. You can write down as many qualities as you like, but don't stop before reaching ten.

Now switch gears and bring into your awareness somebody whom you find repulsive, someone who irritates you, annoys you, aggravates you, or makes you uncomfortable in some way. Start to define those specific qualities that you find unattractive. On the right side of the paper, list ten or more of these undesirable qualities. Why don't you like that person? Why are you infuriated or annoyed by that person? Write down as many qualities as you like, but don't stop before reaching ten.

When you have completed both lists, think again about the person you find attractive and identify at least three unattractive traits in that person. Don't fight it—nobody's perfect. (The more you can accept this in others, the more readily you'll be able to accept it in yourself.) Then think about the person you found unattractive and identify three traits that are relatively appealing.

Now you should have at least twenty-six qualities listed on the page. Read over each one and circle every quality that you own yourself. For example, if you wrote *compassionate* about the attractive person, ask yourself if you are ever compassionate. If so, then circle that word. If not, then don't circle the word. Don't think too much about it—just respond to your first impressions. Go through all words on both lists and circle every word that describes a quality that you can identify in your own nature.

Look at the list again. For every word that you did not circle, identify the ones that are absolutely inapplicable to you, words that definitely do not describe you. Put a checkmark next to those.

Finally, go back and look at the words that you *circled* and identify the top three that describe you most strongly. Turn the paper over and write down those three words. Then go back and look at the words that you *checked* and identify the top three that define you the very least—ones that in no way whatsoever apply to you. Write those three words on the back of the paper under the three words that apply to you the most. Read those six words—the three that describe you best and the three that least apply—out loud. *You are all of these qualities and traits.* The qualities you most strongly deny in yourself are also part of you and are likely the qualities that create the most turbulence in your life. You will attract people with all six of these qualities—the extremely positive qualities because you may not feel that you deserve them and the extremely negative ones because you refuse to acknowledge their presence in your life.

Once you can see yourself in others, it will become much easier to connect with them, and through that connection to discover unity consciousness. The door to synchrodestiny will open. Such is the power of the mirror of relationship.

Exercise 4:
NAMASTE

The Sanskrit word *namaste* (pronounced nah-mah-STAY) means "The spirit in me honors the spirit in you." Whenever you first make eye contact with another person, say "Namaste" silently to yourself. This is a way of acknowledging that the being there is the same as the being here.

When you do this, everything about you—

your body language, your expression, and your tone—will be recognized by the other person at some profound level. Even though this greeting is silent, the other person will consciously or unconsciously register the respect implicit in your greeting. Practice this exercise for a few days, and see if you notice a difference in your interactions with other people.

Sutra Statements
for the Second Principle

Imagine that your spirit is not only in you but in all other beings and everything that is.

(tat tvam asi)

Imagine that everybody is a reflection of yourself.

(tat tvam asi)

Imagine that when you look at the universe you are looking at your mirror.

(tat tvam asi)

Imagine that you see what others see.

(tat tvam asi)

Imagine that you can feel what others feel.

(tat tvam asi)

*Imagine that you are the qualities you most
admire in others.*

(tat tvam asi)

*Imagine that others reflect the qualities you
cherish in yourself.*

(tat tvam asi)

*Imagine that you are a person in a ball of
mirrors where you can see yourself for miles
and every reflection you see is of yourself, but
appears different.*

(tat tvam asi)

10

The Third Principle: Master Your Inner Dialogue

SUTRA: Sat Chit Ananda *(saht chit ah-NAN-dah)*

My inner dialogue reflects the fire of my soul.

The third principle describes how your mind creates your reality—and how, by mastering your inner dialogue, you can literally transform reality to create abundance.

The mantra—*sat chit ananda*—tells us that our soul is that place which is spontaneously love, knowingness, and bliss. *Sat* means truth, freedom from all limitations. *Chit* means total knowledge, spontaneous knowing or pure consciousness. *Ananda* means bliss, total happiness, complete fulfillment.

So what that phrase really says is, "My soul is free from limitations. My soul has spontaneous knowing. My soul exists in complete fulfillment."

Inner dialogue is one of our most basic characteristics. When we meet new people, we're used to looking at how they're dressed, the kind of car they drive, the wristwatch they're wearing. Based on all these external clues, we form an impression of the individual. But this snap judgment is nothing more than the result of the ego having a conversation with itself. That little voice inside your head is constantly assessing this and evaluating that. This inner dialogue has an important function: By making judgments, it contributes to survival. This person may be dangerous. That fruit may be good to eat. This may not be a good time to ask my boss for a raise. Useful though it is, this little voice would have you believe that you and it are one and the same, that its goals are your goals. But as we've seen, there is another place inside you where the silent witness dwells. This is the place where you connect to spirit, where the local mind gives way to the nonlocal mind. This is the place you can access through meditation.

INNER DIALOGUE
AND SELF POWER

Being synchronized with the intelligence field creates balance physically, emotionally, and spiritually. It gives you strength and flexibility that allow you to meet any challenge effortlessly. You become capable of transforming the challenge in such a way that it nourishes you, and you draw greater strength from meeting the challenge.

Our inner dialogue gives us that kind of bright power because it is, in fact, the inner dialogue of the conscious intelligence field. When we are in tune with the universal consciousness, when we are synchronized in the nonlocal intelligence field, we take on the power that emanates from that boundless force. This power comes from within, and when you have it, nothing is beyond your reach.

There are two kinds of power that emanate from the self. The first is the power of agency— the power that comes from having a famous name, lots of money, or an impressive title. The power of agency can be formidable, but it eventually comes to an end. True power comes from within, and it has a spiritual rather than a material foundation. It is permanent and does not die with your body. With agency, identity and power come from some external reference—an object, a situation, a status symbol, a relationship, money. With self-power, identity comes from listening to the true self, and power comes from the internal reference of spirit.

When you work from this internal reference, your sense of self is clear and is not affected by external factors. This is the source of personal power. When external factors fail to influence your sense of self, you become immune to criticism or to praise. You also understand that we are all equal, because we are all connected to the same conscious intelligence flow. That means that you understand that as you move through your life, you are beneath no one and superior to no one. You don't have to beg or plead or convince anyone of anything because you don't have to convince yourself.

As wonderful as this sounds, very few of us actually achieve a state of internal reference. All too often, we muddy the message by allowing our ego to intervene. Our thoughts, influenced by external factors—money worries, job stress, relationship tensions—end up hindering our spiritual development, and we find ourselves moving in a direction opposite from where we want to go.

The two best ways to overcome that tendency are to meditate and to consciously practice positive inner dialogue. Positive inner dialogue helps move us in the right direction, fosters synchronicity, and promotes spiritual development. With positive internal dialogue, we can create self-power.

For example, suppose you are dissatisfied with your job and want to find a new one. You start looking through the newspapers and talking to friends who are familiar with your career, but nothing turns up. You might become frustrated and your inner dialogue might conclude, "There's just nothing out there for me." Observe how that response contrasts with another example from a very different part of the world. Suppose a hunter in the Amazon rain forest is having difficulty finding game. If he goes to a shaman to deal with the situation, neither the hunter nor the shaman looks anywhere but within the hunter himself for the solution to the problem. It never occurs to them to say something like "There's no game out there," because they know there is. The problem is that something within the hunter is preventing him from finding the game. Maybe something in the hunter is even driving away the game. So the shaman asks the hunter to participate in a ritual that is designed to change what is in the hunter's heart and mind—because it is the heart and mind that control the external reality.

When we find ourselves looking at the world and saying, "There's nothing out there for me," we should probably also look into our hearts and ask, "If there's nothing out there, is there anything in here?" We need to examine our inner dialogue to discover where we might be blocking the conscious energy flow, then remove the ego, step out of the way, and let the fire of the soul shine through us.

If you have fire of soul, then Vedic sages say it is reflected in the shining of your eyes. It's reflected spontaneously in your body language and body movements. Everything you think, feel, say, and do will reflect that same fire. How does it look? There are no absolutes, but the spirit is reflected in impeccable speech and behavior, refraining from anything that could potentially be considered hurtful. The spirit is reflected in confidence, happiness, good humor, fearlessness, kindness, and thoughtfulness. The quality of your inner dialogue is instantly obvious to other people, although it might not be recognized for what it is. When you practice positive inner dialogue, people will want to bond with you, help you, be near you. They want to share in the love, knowingness, and bliss that shines through your eyes and is reflected in your every action. This is true inner power.

Exercise 5:

THE FIRE IN YOUR EYES

The fire in your soul will be reflected in your eyes. Whenever you look into a mirror, even if it's just for a second or two, make eye contact with your image and silently repeat the three principles that are the foundation of self-referral. First, say to yourself, "I'm totally independent of the good or bad opinions of others." Second: "I'm beneath no one." Third: "I'm fearless in the face of any and all challenges." Look into your eyes in the mirror and see those attitudes reflected back at you. Just in your eyes, not in your facial expression. Look for

the shine in your eyes to remind yourself of the
fire in your soul.

Sutra Statements
for the Third Principle

Imagine that you are centered and totally at peace.

(sat chit ananda)

Imagine that you are looking at the world with
knowingness and peace.

(sat chit ananda)

Imagine that all beings are your equal.

(sat chit ananda)

Imagine that you are not affected by flattery
or criticism.

(sat chit ananda)

Imagine that you are focused on the journey,
not the destination.

(sat chit ananda)

Imagine that in your presence all hostility is overcome
by a profound peace.

(sat chit ananda)

Imagine that you're detached from the outcome.

(sat chit ananda)

Imagine that a deeply profound ocean of calm exists
in you that is not affected by any turbulence.

(sat chit ananda)

Imagine that love radiates from you like light from a
bonfire.

(sat chit ananda)

Imagine that you are in love with everything and
everybody. Imagine that you are intoxicated
with love.

(sat chit ananda)

Imagine that the right answer comes to you
spontaneously
whenever you are confronted by any question.

(sat chit ananda)

Imagine that you know exactly what to do
in every situation.

(sat chit ananda)

11

The Fourth Principle:
Intent Weaves the
Tapestry of the Universe

SUTRA: San Kalpa *(sahn KAL-pah)*

My intentions have infinite organizing power.

Our intentions are a manifestation of the total universe because we are part of the universe. And our intentions hold within them the mechanics of their fulfillment. All we really need is clarity of intent. Then if we can get the ego out of the way, the intentions fulfill themselves. Our intentions attract the elements and forces, the events, the situations, the circumstances, and the relationships necessary to fulfill the intended outcome. We don't need to become involved in the details—in fact, trying too hard may backfire. Let the nonlocal intelligence synchronize the actions of the universe to fulfill your intentions for you. Intention is a force in nature, like gravity, but more powerful. No one has to concentrate on gravity to make it work. No one can say, "I don't believe in gravity," because it is a force at work in the world whether we understand it or not. Intention works the same way.

As a simple example, think back to a time when you were trying to remember some bit of trivia, a person's name or the title of a book. It was on the tip of your tongue, but you just couldn't quite recall it. Once you try to remember, you've introduced intention. But the harder you try to remember, the farther the information seems to slip away from your conscious recall. But if you eventually take your ego out of the way, and let go of the process of remembering, then your intention goes into the virtual domain, with its infinite organizing power. Even when you've moved on to other thoughts, the virtual domain continues to search for the information, even without your conscious participation. Later, you could be falling asleep, or you could be sitting in a movie, and suddenly the name you were trying so hard to remember simply pops into your awareness. This common example illustrates the way intention works. All we have to do is create the intention and let the universe take over.

The only preparation or participation required

to unleash the power of intention is a connection to the conscious intelligence field, which can be attained many ways, one of the best being meditation. When a person achieves a certain level of consciousness, whatever he or she intends begins to happen. There are people who are so connected with the conscious intelligence field that their every intent manifests itself—the whole order of the universe orchestrates around it. Of course, it is not strictly true that their every personal intention is being met; in actuality, people who are connected with the conscious intelligence field adopt the intentions of the universe. Their intentions are being met, but that's only because the cosmic mind is using their intentions to fulfill its own desires.

We must look for opportunities to exercise intentions, because for the most part our society doesn't provide them. If you're like most people, there won't be many opportunities for going on a retreat to a mountaintop where you can concentrate on the development of your spirit. You are much more likely to have a free moment when you're stuck in traffic or while you're waiting for an important telephone call in your office. Those are more likely opportunities for practicing timeless awareness and spirit-based intention.

Intention is not simply a whim. It requires attention, and it also requires detachment. Once you have created the intention mindfully, you must be able to detach from the outcome, and let the universe handle the details of fulfillment. If you don't, ego gets involved and clouds the process. You'll feel frustrated if your intention isn't realized soon enough. Your sense of self-importance may be threatened, or perhaps you'll start feeling sorry for yourself. Intent in nature orchestrates its own fulfillment. The only thing that could interfere is domination by your own ego needs and totally selfish concerns.

Of course, the best way to have all your intentions realized is to align your intentions with the cosmic intent, to create harmony between what you intend and what the universe intends for you. Once that congruence comes into being, you'll find that synchronicity takes on a larger role in your life. The best way to create that harmony is by nurturing an attitude of simple gratitude. Acknowledge your gratitude for everything in your life. Give thanks for your place in the cosmos and for the opportunity you have to further the destiny we all share. Part of creating harmony involves abandoning grievances of all kinds. Grievance comes from the ego. Animals don't have any problems with grudges or grievances. It's only among us human beings that intention is so often encumbered by all sorts of emotional baggage. You must let all that go in order to create a pure intention.

Exercise 6:

FOCUSING INTENTION

The best way to focus on intentions is to write them down. Although this may sound like an obvious first step, it is a step that many people ignore. As a result, their intentions often remain unfocused, and therefore unrealized.

Go to a quiet place where you are not likely to be disturbed. Write down what you want on all different levels of desire. Include material, ego gratification, relationship, self-esteem, and spiritual desires. Be as specific as possible.

Ask yourself what you want on the material level, in terms of abundance and affluence. Do you want to own your own house with four bedrooms? Write that down. Do you want to be able to send your children to college? Write that down. Think also of your desires for sensory gratification—sound, touch, sight, taste, smell, and sensuality—anything that gratifies the senses. Write those down.

Ask yourself what you want in terms of relationships. Write down your desires for all your relationships—romantic partners, children, peers, parents, friends, and professional relationships.

Write down what you want in terms of personal accomplishments or recognition. Note what you want on a more universal level—how can you help? What do you want to do with your life in terms of your society, your country, your civilization?

What do you want to contribute? Write down what you want when you think of discovering your highest sense of self. Whom do you want to be? What spiritually do you want to add to your life? Write down everything you desire on a single sheet of paper. Add or subtract from the list as your desires change or become fulfilled.

Meditate on what life would be like if all these desires were to manifest. See if you can create inner visions of genuine fulfillment on both material and spiritual levels. Don't be concerned about having these visions in any kind of order, or whether they're very realistic or not. Just see them all happening—feel them with all your five senses. The goal is to have congruent attention on all these four levels of aspiration. When that kind of congruency is in play, the internal dialogue is very powerful and clear, and will help you gain unity of consciousness.

Intentions do not need constant attention, but they do need to remain focused. This is a habit that you develop over time. Look at your list once or twice during the day. Read it over again just before you meditate. When you go into meditation, you silence the self. The ego disappears. As a result, you detach from the results and outcomes, you don't get involved in the details, and you let the infinite organizing power of the deeper intelligence orchestrate and fulfill all the details of your intentions for you. The key is to move away from the level of the ego, away from the level of the self and self-esteem, to let the nonlocal intelligence orchestrate the fulfillment of your desires through synchronicity.

In the beginning, you can be as selfish as you want. In the beginning your intentions may be all about "self" and the little details of what you want to happen in your life. But eventually you will realize that the goal is fulfillment at all levels, not just the personal or ego level. As you start to see the fulfillment of your intentions, your self-interest will diminish because you know you can have it all. When you have enough food to eat, you don't obsess about eating all the time. It's the same with intentions. When you know that fulfillment is possible, you will think less about your personal needs and more about the needs of the rest of the world. This is a process that works through stages. Be patient, but watch for the miracles to begin.

Exercise 7:

THE HEART SUTRA

This is a meditation exercise that demonstrates the power of intention. But it is more than a mere demonstration. Do this regularly so that this ritual can focus your attention and your intention.

Go to a quiet place where you are not likely to be disturbed for fifteen minutes. Close your eyes, practice the primordial sound mantra—"so-hum"—for five minutes, placing your awareness on your breath.

After five minutes, put your mental awareness in the area of your heart, in the middle of your chest. With your attention on your heart, you may begin to feel your heart beating more strongly. This is normal. As you experience the beating of your heart, begin to also experience gratitude. The way to experience gratitude is to think of all the things, events, and relationships in your life for which you have reason to be grateful. Allow those images to surface in your consciousness while you keep your attention on your heart. Take a moment to think of all the people whom you love and all the people who share their love with you.

Then say to yourself: *"Every decision I make is a choice between a grievance and a miracle. I let go of grievances and choose miracles."* Certain resentments and grievances—and the people associated with those resentments and grievances—may surface in your awareness. If they do, just say, *"I let go of the grievances. I choose the miracles."* Then become aware of your heart again, and consciously start to breathe into your heart. As you do, say to yourself, "Love . . . knowingness . . . bliss . . . love," and then breathe out for the same count of four. Between each inhalation and exhalation pause for several seconds. Do this for three or four minutes.

Through the heart sutra meditation, the fire of

your soul—which is love, knowingness, and bliss—will start to broadcast itself through the heart. This is where the third principle of synchrodestiny meets the fourth principle: The fire of your soul now begins to create your intention.

After having said "I let go of grievances and choose miracles" a few times, start to repeat mentally the phrase *"Thy will be done."* This prepares your mind to receive the intention of the nonlocal intelligence, and to understand that it is, simultaneously, your intention.

After about a minute, let go of all thoughts and bring your awareness fully to your heart. Experience your heartbeat, either as a sound or as a sensation. Feel it throbbing. Once you can sense your heart, transfer your awareness into your hands, and feel the throbbing of your heart in your hands. Introduce the intention to increase the blood flow to your hands. Just have the intention. As the blood flow to your hands increases, either the throbbing will increase or you'll feel warmth, tingling, or some other sensation. Introduce the intention of increasing warmth so that your hands become warmer and warmer. Feel the warmth in your hands as your intention alone increases the blood flow.

When your hands have become warm, move your awareness into your face, the upper part of your face around the eyeballs, and have the same intention. Increase the blood flow to your face so your face starts to flush and get warm. Just have the intention. You may feel a pulsing or tingling sensation around your eyes as the blood flow increases and your face becomes warm.

Finally, bring your awareness back into your heart. Imagine that there is a pinpoint of light pulsating in your heart, matching your heartbeat. This pinpoint of light pulsating in your heart is the light of your soul and it pulsates with the three qualities of the soul: love, knowingness, and bliss, or *sat chit ananda*, which is also the sutra for the Third Principle in Chapter 10. As it pulsates, experience the pinpoint of love, knowingness, bliss. It is sending radiant light to the rest of your body. Slowly let that pinpoint of light fade away from your awareness, and tune in to your whole body. Feel the sensations. Then open your eyes. The meditation is over.

Sutra Statements for the Fourth Principle

Imagine that the whole universe is a vast ocean of consciousness, and your intentions shoot out from within your heart and ripple across the vast ocean of consciousness.

(san kalpa)

Imagine that your intention is orchestrating the infinite activity of the universe, counterbalancing the whole ecosystem.

(san kalpa)

Imagine that your intention can heal those who are not well.

(san kalpa)

Imagine that your intention can bring joy and laughter to those who are in sorrow.

(san kalpa)

Imagine that you can bring success to those who are failing.

(san kalpa)

Imagine that you can bring strength to those who feel weak and fearful.

(san kalpa)

Imagine that you can bring hope to those who are feeling helpless.

(san kalpa)

Imagine that your thoughts affect the natural forces of the universe, that you can bring rain and sunshine, clouds and rainbows.

(san kalpa)

Imagine that every thought you have, every word you utter, every deed of yours brings some benefit to the world.

(san kalpa)

12

The Fifth Principle: Harness Your Emotional Turbulence

SUTRA: Moksha *(MOKE-shah)*

I am emotionally free.

Once we understand that external reality can't be separated from internal reality, once we understand that the universe really is our extended body, it becomes very clear that negative energy within ourselves is destructive. Emotional turbulence is a major barrier to the spontaneous fulfillment of desire, but it is possible to transform negative energy into a higher level of awareness.

The word *moksha* means "freedom." As this sutra resonates within you, it expresses "I am emotionally free. My soul is disengaged from melodrama. I am free from resentment, grievances, hostility, and guilt. I am free of self-importance. I am free of self-concern. I'm free of self-pity. I can laugh at myself. I see the humor in life." These are all contained in that freedom; if I'm not emotionally free, then I overshadow and cloud the experience of the spirit with the ego, and my best intentions cannot be fulfilled.

Ultimately emotional freedom leads to psychological and spiritual freedom as well. There are really only two emotions: pleasure and pain—either it feels good or it hurts. Most people believe that the two fundamental emotions are love and fear, but these are really just the ways we respond to the potential for pleasure and pain. *Love* means we want to get closer to it because we think it will bring us pleasure. *Fear* means we want to move away because we think it will bring pain.

We spend our lives seeking pleasure and avoiding pain. The things that bring pleasure or pain are different for each of us. Pleasure and pain flow from the needs that you have. If I have a craving for chocolate ice cream, and you bring me chocolate ice cream, then I interpret that as being pleasurable. If you have an allergy to chocolate and someone brings you chocolate ice cream, that gift is associated with pain. It's all about perception and interpretation. It's the ego that interprets things as being pleasurable or painful, and the ego experiences any crossing of the boundary of ego without permission as being painful.

The optimal and truest condition is one of balance. Any time we have emotional turbulence, we upset our natural internal balance, which can block our spiritual evolution and may even disconnect us from synchronicity. This is not to say that emotions are, in themselves, harmful or to be avoided. As human beings we will always have emotions; these are part of the human condition. But extremes of emotion will set us off course for our true life purpose. There will always be events or relationships in our lives that trigger strong emotions in us. There will always be things in this world that cause great pain or anxiety. But we need to avoid getting stuck on one emotion.

Think of life as a river with two banks—pleasure on one side, pain on the other. The best way to float down that river is to stay in the middle, moving evenly between the two banks. If you stray too close to either side, your passage slows, and you run the risk of running aground. Too much pleasure leads to addiction. Too much pain can eclipse your enjoyment of life.

It is important to note that pain does not have to be physical. It can be emotional pain, or even the memory of a past pain. Although our natural instinct is to avoid pain, we must deal with it when it occurs; otherwise, it will resurface later in life in some form of emotional turbulence. The form it takes may be different from what you expect, but it will resurface, perhaps as insomnia, or illness, or anxiety, or depression.

Perhaps the most destructive emotion is anger. The ultimate goal of spiritual transformation is enlightenment, the perpetual state of unity consciousness, the constant awareness that you and I and all the rest of the universe are patterns of the same fabric, woven of nonlocal intelligence. Anger motivates us to harm others, moving us in the opposite direction from enlightenment and unity consciousness. Anger clouds any perception of unity. Anger is about only the ego. Rather than moving you forward toward synchronicity and enlightenment, anger pushes you backward, closing you down to the transformative messages of the universe.

It is therefore critically important to control this form of emotional turbulence. Venting anger really does not help. Venting simply gives fuel to the anger and allows it to grow. Angry feelings need to be dealt with in a positive way as soon as possible after they arise. The goal is not to fuel the anger, or to try to smother it by burying it. Instead, we must convert the anger, or any other destructive emotion, within ourselves.

The first step to converting emotions is to take responsibility for what you are feeling. In order to take responsibility, you must recognize the emotion. What are you feeling? Where do you feel it in your body? Once you can identify the feeling, witness it. Experience it as objectively as possible, as though you are another person looking in. Anger is triggered by pain. Describe the pain from this objective point of view.

After the pain is identified in these ways, you can begin to express, release, and share the pain. Transform the painful experience into new awareness. Eventually you may even be able to celebrate the pain as another step on your road to spiritual enlightenment. When you embrace the pain in this way, emotional turbulence will disappear and the path to synchronicity again becomes clear.

Exercise 8:

DEALING WITH PAIN

This exercise will require about ten minutes of quiet time in a place where you are not likely to be disturbed. Begin by meditating for a few moments.

With your eyes closed, recall some event or situation in the past that was very upsetting to you. It may have been an argument, or some time when your feelings were hurt, or some random encounter that made you angry. Once you've settled on an upsetting situation, try to recall as many details about it as possible. Create a mental movie of exactly what happened.

The first step to dealing with the pain of this situation is to identify exactly what you are feeling. What word best describes how you feel because of this event or situation? Try to come up with a single word that encompasses as many of the feelings as possible, your best description. Now, focus on that word for a few seconds.

Let your attention gradually shift from that word to your body. What physical sensations are you feeling as a result of reliving that emotion? Every emotion has both mental and physical aspects that cannot be separated. Our feelings occur both in our minds and in our bodies at the same instant. Feel the sensations that this incident you are thinking about has created. Have your hands automatically clenched into fists? Do you feel a tightening of your stomach? A pain in your gut? Notice the physical experience of the emotion, and localize it to a specific spot on your body.

The next step is to express the feeling. Place your hand on the part of your body where you sense that the feeling is located. Out loud, say, "It hurts here." If there is more than one location for the pain, touch each place and repeat the phrase, "It hurts here."

For every emotional hurt, we have the power within us to make the pain disappear. Our reactions to external events localize in our bodies. We create emotions, which create physical pain. When we understand that simple fact, we can learn to change the way we respond to outside events. We can choose the way we react to incidents in the world. If we react with anger, hostility, depression, anxiety, or another intense emotion, our bodies follow along and create the necessary hormones and muscle contractions and other physical manifestations that eventually cause us actual pain. Therefore, we must always remember that these effects are our responsibility in the sense that we can change our reactions in ways that are less personally harmful. We can become free of emotional drama and turbulence. Meditate for a moment on the concept of personal responsibility for emotional reactions.

Once the pain has been located and acknowledged, and after you've taken responsibility for it, you can release the pain. Place your attention on the part of your body where you are holding the pain. With every exhalation of breath, have the intention of releasing that tension that you are holding. For half a minute, focus on releasing tension and pain with every breath. Let it go. Breathe it out.

The next step is to share the pain. Imagine that you could speak to the person who was involved in the incident that you have recalled for this exercise. What would you say to that person? As you consider this, remember that the person was not the true cause of your pain. You had the emotional reaction that manifested in physical pain. You have taken responsibility. Knowing this, what would you say to that person? What you choose to say will be personal to you and your situation. Whatever you say to share the pain you experienced will help to cleanse the experience from your consciousness forever. Share what you felt, share how you feel now, and share how you intend to deal with such feelings in the future.

This exercise can be used whenever you feel emotional turbulence in your life. When you have completed the exercise, take a moment to celebrate that you have used this painful experience to transcend to a higher level of consciousness. If you use this exercise consistently, you will eventually be able to entirely free yourself of emotional turbulence and pain, freeing your way to experience synchronicity.

Exercise 9:

NONVIOLENT COMMUNICATION

There will always be situations and circumstances in your life when someone will cross some personal boundary, triggering strong emotional responses. This exercise is derived from Marshall Rosenberg's excellent book *Nonviolent Communication*.

There are four basic steps to nonviolent communication, which involve four questions you ask yourself whenever you find yourself becoming defensive. When someone pushes your buttons, it's tempting to want to push back. But that is not an optimal response—it is not productive, it wastes valuable personal energy, and it creates more turbulence in the world. For this exercise, think of a recent situation when something irritated or upset you in some way. Keeping that experience in mind, follow these four steps.

Separate Observation from Evaluation

Define what actually happened, instead of relying on your interpretation of what happened. Be as objective as possible when describing the event. Ask yourself: What are you actually responding to? What actually occurred? What did you see and hear?

For example, you may be driving along in the car, wondering whether you need anything for dinner tonight when your spouse notices your silence and asks, "What are you upset about?" You say, "I'm not upset about anything, I was just thinking about dinner." Your spouse responded to your silence with an evaluation, not an observation. Any time you attach meaning to an action, that is an interpretation or evaluation. For the following sets of sentences, see if you can figure out which is the evaluation and which is the observation:

1. *"I saw you flirting with that woman at the party."*
2. *"I saw you talking with that woman at the party for more than an hour."*

1. *"I can see that your work has become more important to you than your family."*
2. *"You have been leaving for work before dawn and coming home after 10 P.M. every day for the last three weeks."*

1. *"You don't love me anymore."*
2. *"You don't kiss me when you come home from work anymore."*

In all three sets, the first statement is the interpretation or evaluation.

Whenever you find yourself responding with an emotional reaction, stop for a moment and try to discern the difference between your interpretation of the event and the objective observation of the event. Observations are empowering because they allow us to recognize how much of our response to others is based on interpretation, which in turn allows us to change our patterns of responding to the actions of others.

STEP 2:
Define Your Feelings

Think to yourself, What feelings arose as a result of the situation? What am I feeling? As you describe your feelings, use language that reflects only the feelings that you are responsible for and avoid words that victimize you. For example, you might feel appreciated, angry, antagonistic, anxious, afraid, bold, beautiful, confident, blissful, bewildered, glad, free, exhilarated, calm, astonished, cheerful, eager, hopeful, joyful, optimistic, proud, radiant, relaxed, sensitive, ashamed, bored, confused, dejected, disgruntled, displeased, dull, fatigued, guilty, hostile, irate, jealous, lazy, or lonely.

Avoid words that require another person to "make" you feel a certain way. For example, you cannot feel "attacked" by yourself—that emotion does not arise from you but from your response to another. Other words to avoid: *abandoned, abused, betrayed, cheated, coerced, diminished, manipulated, misunderstood, overworked, rejected, unheard, unseen, unsupported.* When you use these words to identify your feelings, this means that you are giving others too much power over your emotions. If so, you'll tend to attract people who evoke these feelings, and get caught in a vicious cycle. It's very difficult to be happy until you start owning your own emotions.

STEP 3:

State Your Needs Clearly

Ask yourself, What do I need in this situation? You wouldn't be having strong feelings if all your needs were being met. Identify the need as specifically as possible. Start with your gut reaction;

then work your way down the chain of desires until you find some specific examples of things to ask for. For example, "I need to feel loved. Why?" "I feel lonely—I need to feel less alone. Why?" "I don't have close friends—I need to find some friends and develop relationships." This line of thought eventually leads to something you can ask of another person. You cannot ask another person to make you feel loved; that is beyond anyone's capability. But you can ask another person to go out to a movie with you, to come to a party, to have a cup of coffee.

STEP 4:

Ask, Don't Demand

Once we identify a need and are ready to make a request, we often demand rather than request that our needs be met. Demands are less likely to be fulfilled because people inherently respond poorly to demands. Most people, however, are happy to fulfill a request.

For example, instead of demanding, "Pick up the dry cleaning," you'll be more likely to get a positive response if you ask, "Would you please pick up the dry cleaning?"

In addition, as in step 3, you'll want to ask for a particular specific behavior. The more specific the behavior, the more likely it is that your request will be answered. For example, instead of saying, "Love me forever," you might ask, "Will you marry me?" Instead of asking the general question, "Can we spend more time together?" you might ask, "Can we go to the park this afternoon?"

*T*hese steps are helpful in all situations, but they are especially helpful if there's a conflict. Whenever you are part of a tense situation, allow yourself to take a step back from the emotions of the moment and choose conscious communication. What do you observe? How does it make you feel? Determine your need. Make a request. This should help short-circuit a potentially volatile situation and allow you to maintain your equanimity—or at least regain it.

Exercise 10:

HEALING CHILDHOOD ANGER

For this exercise, you will need approximately ten minutes of uninterrupted time.

Think back to yesterday. Imagine that your memory is a videocassette that you can rewind to any time you choose. Right now, take it back just twenty-four hours. What were some of the things you did during the day? Did anything frighten you or make you angry? It doesn't have to be anything especially important or dramatic—you may have felt impatient waiting in line, or you might have witnessed someone being rude or inconsiderate. For the next minute or so, try to remember the events of the day in as much detail as you can. Focus on a moment of anger, becoming aware of the sensations in your body as well as the emotions in your mind.

Next, rewind that videotape back even farther. Think back exactly one year. Try to recall what you were doing a year ago on this date, or as close to it as you can remember. What was on your mind at that time? Do you recall being worried or angry about something? Try to feel the emotions of that time in your mind and in your body. Are the feelings the same as the feelings you remember feeling yesterday?

Rewind the tape even farther back to when you were a teenager. Again, focus on a situation that made you angry or frightened. Relive the feelings, mentally and physically. Notice how the anger that you experienced yesterday has been built on emotions from so long ago.

Try now to remember an incident from childhood. What is the earliest time in your life that you can recall being really angry? Bring that experience into your awareness. Where were you when it happened? Who else was there? Who or what was it that made you so angry? Feel all the sensations created by that anger.

Notice how the fear and anger have accumulated over the years. Although you cannot remember it, there was a time in your life before you ever felt anger or fear, a time of total peace and tranquillity. Try to imagine what that experience of utter bliss might have been like. Focus on a time before fear or anger. Rewind that imaginary tape of your life until the screen goes black, and feel the boundaries evaporate between yourself and your surroundings. For the next minute, feel the total loss of all your accumulated anger, fear, and ego.

With that feeling of total bliss still in your awareness, begin to move that imaginary videotape forward again. Visit the same points in your life that you stopped at earlier—those angry or fearful moments from your childhood, your teenage years, a year ago, yesterday. As you envision these scenes again, introduce the experience of bliss back into the setting. Instead of allowing one moment of anger to build upon another, begin to erase these moments one by one, from earliest childhood to just yesterday. Spend a minute or so feeling the anger and fear being erased by this memory of bliss. And as those feelings are erased, allow the toxic buildup of years of anger and fear to be erased from your spirit.

You can use this exercise at any time to attack the anger problem at its roots. Many people find it especially useful at night, just before they go to sleep, so they wake up blissful and without residual anger.

Sutra Statements
for the Fifth Principle

Imagine that you are without physical form,
a field of awareness everywhere at all times.

(moksha)

Imagine that you have left behind forever any
sense of anger or resentment.

(moksha)

Imagine that you are free from blaming, free
from feeling blame and guilt.

(moksha)

Imagine that you are never drawn into melodrama
or hysteria.

(moksha)

Imagine that you can choose any emotional feeling
you want to experience.

(moksha)

Imagine that you can set any goal you want to
achieve and actually achieve it.

(moksha)

*Imagine that you are free of your habitual
compulsions and patterns of behavior.*

(moksha)

Imagine that you are free of any addictions.

(moksha)

Imagine that you never participate in any gossip.

(moksha)

*Imagine that you are free to respond at the
highest level, no matter what the situation is
or how anyone else behaves.*

(moksha)

*Imagine that there are no limitations to what
you can manifest.*

(moksha)

*Imagine that you can see infinite possibilities
at all times.*

(moksha)

13

The Sixth Principle: Celebrate the Dance of the Cosmos

SUTRA: Shiva-Shakti *(SHE-vah SHOCK-tee)*

I am giving birth to the gods and goddesses inside me;
they express all their attributes and powers through me.

The sixth principle encourages us to live life
fully by embracing both the masculine and the
feminine aspects of our being.

One way to embrace both aspects of your self is
to call upon both masculine and feminine archetypes. According to Carl Jung, archetypes are
inherited memories represented in the mind as universal symbols, and can be observed in dreams and
myths. They are states of awareness. Archetypes
are universal concentrations of psychic energy.

Archetypes exist as potential and lie dormant in your consciousness. Everyone has at least one archetype, which stays dormant until triggered by some situation in the environment or in the conscious or unconscious mental life of a person. Once triggered, the archetype will manifest its powers and attributes through you. What you do with your life is usually a representation to some extent of the combination of your archetypes. For example, a person who wields exceptional power in the world, such as a king or a president, will likely have Zeus or Hera as archetypes of power and leadership. But if that person is also exceptionally wise, he or she might also have Athena as an archetype of wisdom.

It is possible to consciously trigger your archetype through intent. Once you discover your primary archetypes, you can begin to call them to you daily. Surround yourself with symbols, words, or representations that remind you of your archetypes. With such symbols next to your bed, let these be the first things you look at when you wake up in the morning. Ask your archetypes for their guidance and wisdom, and ask that they become part of you and work through you. This can be as simple as saying, "I ask that you become part of me and work through me. Guide me through my life."

If you invite your archetypes in this way just after your daily meditation, you will start to feel their presence more strongly and more directly.

They can provide access to the hidden strengths within you.

Exercise 11:
FINDING THE COSMOS WITHIN

Read this into a tape and play it to yourself.

Sit or lie comfortably with your eyes closed. Quiet your internal dialogue by observing your breath.

After a few minutes put your attention on your heart. Visualize your heart as a pulsating sphere of light. In this sphere visualize two or three divine beings or archetypal energies. These could be angels, gods, or goddesses. Now visualize the rest of your body also as a body of light. Now slowly imagine this light body with its pulsating sphere of divine beings expanding so it fills the entire room in which you are sitting or lying. Allow the expansion to occur beyond the confines of the room so that you are no longer in the room but in fact the room is in you. Continue the process of expanding your light body so that the entire city in which you live exists in your being—the buildings, the people, the traffic, and the countryside.

Continue to expand your sense of self to include in your physical being the state in which you live, your country, and ultimately the entire planet. Now see that the whole world exists in you—all the people, all other sentient beings, trees and forests, rivers and mountains, rainfall and sunshine, earth and water—these are different components of your being, just like different organs in your body.

Now quietly say to yourself, "I am not in the world; the world is in me." Whatever imbalances you see in this world of yours, ask the divine beings still dancing in your pulsating sphere of a heart to correct them. Ask these divine beings to fulfill any desire you have and to bring harmony, beauty, healing, and joy to the different parts of your cosmic self. Continue to expand your sense of self to include planets and moons, stars and galaxies.

Now say to yourself, "I am not in the universe; the universe is in me." Slowly begin to diminish the size of your cosmic self until you can once again experience your personal body. Imagine trillions of cells in your personal body—all part of a dance, each cell an entire universe unto itself. Remind yourself that your true being inhabits all these levels of creation, from microcosm to macrocosm, from the atom to the universe, from your personal body to your cosmic body. Remind yourself that at each of these levels of your existence you have available to you the divine energies that nonlocally orchestrate the cosmic dance to create the harmonious interaction of elements and forces that can fulfill any desire. Express your gratitude to these archetypal energies.

Now just remain sitting or lying quietly, feeling

all the sensations in your body. You may feel tingling or exhilaration. After two or three minutes, open your eyes. The exercise is over.

Sutra Statements for the Sixth Principle

Imagine that you are a shape-shifter.
(Shiva-Shakti)

Imagine that you can be both masculine and feminine if you choose.
(Shiva-Shakti)

Imagine that you are strong, decisive, courageous, articulate, and powerful.
(Shiva-Shakti)

Imagine that you are beautiful, sexual, intuitive, nurturing, and affectionate.
(Shiva-Shakti)

Imagine that you are as stable as a mountain.
(Shiva-Shakti)

Imagine that you are as flexible as the wind.
(Shiva-Shakti)

Imagine that you are an angel with wings.
(Shiva-Shakti)

*Imagine that you are an enlightened being with
infinite compassion.*
(Shiva-Shakti)

*Imagine that you are a divine being of God
playing in celestial realms.*
(Shiva-Shakti)

*Imagine once again that you are a shape-shifter,
that you can become any animal, any bird, any
insect, any plant, or even a rock.*
(Shiva-Shakti)

*Imagine that all the mythical beings reside
in you, although there are some that are
your favorite archetypes.*
(Shiva-Shakti)

*Imagine that you can become the heroes and
heroines you most admire.*
(Shiva-Shakti)

14

The Seventh Principle:
Accessing the Conspiracy
of Improbabilities

SUTRA: Ritam *(REE-tahm)*

I am alert, awake to coincidences, and know that they are messages from God. I flow with the cosmic dance.

The seventh principle incorporates all the other aspects of synchrodestiny to form an approach to life that comes from peaceful awareness.

Ritam means "I am alert to the conspiracy of improbabilities."

Every event has a particular likelihood of happening, or probability. The probability of winning the lottery is very low. The probability of winning the lottery without buying a ticket is even lower.

We maximize the probability that something will happen by our actions. And many of our actions are determined by our karmic conditioning—those interpretations of past experiences and relationships that form and affect our life's memories and desires. If we have had past experiences of being lucky, the probability of buying a lottery ticket increases. But a person who has never won anything feels defeated even before the ticket is purchased, and may never buy the ticket at all.

In order to change your life, therefore, you must break free of your present karmic conditioning. You've got to change your interpretation of what happens in your life. You must transform yourself into the person for whom the probability of great things happening increases. And this transformation starts at the level of the soul. The soul gives meaning to events. The soul takes actions by influencing our minds. And for every action, there is a memory, an interpretation. Meaning, experience, interpretation, memory, desire—all of these are very closely connected through the karmic cycle.

We get used to a certain way of doing things and continue that pattern out of habit, simply because it is comfortable. In order to change your life, you have to find a way to break the pattern.

This is not easy, but people do it every day. The best way is to watch for signs of new probabilities—and those signs come to us in the form of coincidences.

Coincidences are messages from the nonlocal domain, invitations to break our karmic bonds. Coincidences invite us to relinquish the known and embrace the unknown. A coincidence is a creative, quantum leap in the behavior of the universe itself. Since the known is itself a habit of past conditioning, creativity and freedom exist in the unknown—anything that breaks through the probability amplitude set by karma. That is why it is important to look for coincidences, to keep a record of them. When you notice coincidences, you can discover their hidden meanings for your life.

A coincidence is, by definition, a synchronistic experience. It comes from the nonlocal domain, and affects our world in unpredictable ways. The very fact that it's a coincidence means that it is a message from God. We must take heed, and then take action. This is our opportunity for a creative response. The goal of enlightenment is to go beyond the probability pattern and experience true freedom. This is why it is important to never ignore a coincidence. Never pass up a chance to see what the universe has planned for you. And if you pay attention to coincidences, you'll find that they accelerate, creating even more opportunities.

This is the secret of synchrodestiny. All the ideas presented here are the ruling principles of the universe. If you make them the guideposts of your own life, you live the life of your dreams. Understanding that these principles are not just abstractions, that actually they are operating in everything we do, is really more than just awareness: It's really a kind of celebration. When you have mastered synchrodestiny, when you have learned to synchronize your life with the universe itself, you are celebrating the cosmic dance.

Exercise 12:

PUTTING IT ALL TOGETHER

Go to a place where a lot of activity is taking place, such as a shopping mall. Buy something to eat from the food court. Sit on a bench. Close your eyes. With full awareness, taste the food, smell its aroma, and feel its texture. While keeping your eyes closed, pay attention to all the sounds in your environment. What's that music in the background? Christmas carols? The theme song of a movie? Can you tune in to the conversation of the people next to you? Can you hear scattered phrases, words? Do any sounds strike you as attractive, or draw your attention more than others?

Now put your awareness in your body; feel everything around you. The hardness or softness of the bench or sofa—is it wood, or metal, or fabric?

Now open your eyes and observe the scene around you, the people walking, the colors, the shops, the items in the windows, and the art galleries.

Now close your eyes and in your imagination note once again what you have experienced—the tastes, the smells, the textures, the colors and the objects you saw, the sounds you heard. Now pick an item from each of your sensory experiences. An example of these might include the following: strawberry ice cream on your tongue, the smell of baking bread, the touch of craggy rocks under your feet, a beautiful painting of the sun setting over hills, Christmas carols, and the theme song from the James Bond movie *Goldfinger*. Now tell yourself that all these sounds, smells, textures, and tastes are part of a story. Ask yourself what the story is. Ask your nonlocal self to reveal the story to you. Now let go and assume that your nonlocal self will provide the answer in the form of a synchronistic experience.

The exercise above is an actual example of an experience I had at a shopping mall during Christmastime. One year later I was in Jamaica. I had taken a drive into the countryside. I saw a scene very similar to the picture in the painting—a beautiful sunset over a hill by the ocean. Upon inquiry I learned that this place was called Strawberry Hill and the James Bond movie *Goldfinger* had been shot here. There was a beautiful hotel on Strawberry Hill. I decided to go inside. They had a luxurious spa. The spa director was delighted to meet me, and he told me that he had been looking for me for the last several weeks because he wanted advice on Ayurvedic therapies. We ended up talking about a mutual collaboration. Several years later I also met the owner of the hotel, who was a record company executive. His wife had an illness for which she consulted me, and we became close friends. He helped me with great advice when I produced my first music CD with healing meditations. Many years later our friendships have continued to evolve, and we feel bonded to each other in the spirit of love; we know we are karmically connected.

Sutra Statements
for the Seventh Principle

Imagine that you move in rhythm with the
impulses of a conscious universe.

(ritam)

Imagine that you dance to the rhythm
of the universe.

(ritam)

Imagine that your body's rhythms are
in perfect order.

(ritam)

Imagine that your body is a symphony.

(ritam)

Imagine that you are the harmony of the universe.

(ritam)

Imagine that every time you seek something, the
universe provides clues in the form of coincidences.

(ritam)

Imagine that there is a connection between what
happens in your dreams and what happens in your
waking life.

(ritam)

Imagine that you are transforming and
evolving into a higher being.

(ritam)

Imagine that there is meaning and purpose to
everything that happens and everything you do.

(ritam)

*Imagine that you have a contribution to
make to the world.*

(ritam)

Imagine that life is full of coincidences.

(ritam)

Imagine that you notice what others may not notice.

(ritam)

*Imagine that you see the hidden meaning
behind events.*

(ritam)

Imagine that life is full of peak experiences.

(ritam)

*Imagine that you have unique talents that
you use to serve and help others.*

(ritam)

*Imagine that all your relationships are
nurturing and playful.*

(ritam)

Imagine that you delight in play and humor.

(ritam)

Living Synchrodestiny

15

I'd like to return again to the question I asked at the beginning of the book: If you knew that miracles could happen, what miracles would you wish for?

Most people dream first of having enough money. Having a billion dollars in the bank would certainly mean less financial anxiety. We tend to think that once we have that kind of security, then we would be free to choose the life that makes us happiest, that fulfills our inner needs, that marks our stay on earth as valuable in some way. If you knew you could have it all and do anything you wanted, what would you choose to have and what would you choose to do?

Synchrodestiny allows you to make these miracles happen, without limits, without end. And it does this by gently and progressively nudging you from the local to the nonlocal domain. When we live only in the local domain, we are impoverished. Our spiritual bank accounts are empty. In the local domain, where most of us reside all the time, you can never be sure of what's going to happen next. Are you going to make it through the day, the week, the month? Here your actions will carry the burden of anxiety. Your thoughts will be clouded with doubt, and your intentions will be blocked by ego concerns.

But using synchrodestiny to get in touch with the nonlocal domain allows you to enter into a realm of infinite creativity and infinite correlation. Here you have inner security; you are free of anxiety, and free to be the person you were meant to be. You have the spiritual equivalent of a billion dollars in the bank. In the nonlocal domain you have an unlimited supply of knowledge, of inspiration, of creativity, of potential. You have access to an infinite supply of everything the universe has to offer. Whatever else happens in your life, you are calm, secure, and infinitely blessed.

The principles of synchrodestiny offer a direct route to developing your connection with the nonlocal domain. Practice meditation and review the daily Sutra Statements, and in time you will find yourself connected with spirit in a way that makes miracles not only possible, but a natural part of your everyday life.

Like any other worthwhile journey, living synchrodestiny will require some sacrifice on your part. You need to sacrifice your mistaken ideas that the world operates like a well-oiled machine without consciousness. You need to sacrifice your notion that you are alone in the world. You need to sacrifice the myth that a magical life is not possible. Some people live magical lives all the time. They have learned how to get back in touch with the boundless energy that lies at the heart of the universe. They have learned to watch for clues to the intention of the nonlocal expressed through coincidences, and to derive meaning from those clues so they know what actions are needed to increase the probability that wondrous things will happen.

SYNCHRODESTINY AND STATES OF CONSCIOUSNESS

According to Vedanta, there are seven states of consciousness, but many of them have not been thoroughly investigated by modern medical researchers. Indeed, some of them are not even recognized by mainstream science. In India, one of the greatest seers of the twentieth century, Sri Aurobindo, said that because we are in a very early stage of human evolution, most of us experience only the first three states of consciousness: sleeping, dreaming, and wakefulness. Eventually we will recognize and understand the more expanded states of consciousness, and when we do, such concepts as synchronicity, telepathy, clairvoyance, and knowledge of past lives will become commonly accepted.

Each of the seven states of consciousness represents an increase in our experience of synchronicity, and each progressive state moves us closer to the ideal of enlightenment. Everyone commonly experiences the first three. Unfortunately, most people never move beyond these three basic states.

The first level of consciousness is deep sleep. In deep sleep there is some awareness—we still respond to stimuli such as sound, bright light, or touch—but mostly our senses are dulled and there is very little cognition or perception.

The second state of consciousness is dreaming. During dreams, we are a little more awake and a little more alert than during deep sleep. When we dream, we are having experiences. We see images; we hear sounds. We even think in our dreams. While we are dreaming, the world of our dreams seems real, important, and relevant. It's only after we wake up that we recognize the dream as a reality that was confined to that particular moment when we were dreaming and perhaps not directly relevant like our waking life.

The third state of consciousness is being awake. This is the state most of us are in most of the time. Measurable brain activity during the waking state of consciousness is quite different when compared with brain activity during both deep sleep and dreaming.

The fourth state of consciousness occurs when we actually glimpse the soul, when we transcend, when we become, even for a fraction of a moment, absolutely still and quiet and become aware of the observer inside us. This state of consciousness occurs during meditation, when we experience the gap, that quiet moment between our thoughts. People who meditate regularly have this experience every time they meditate. As a result, their state of self expands.

The fourth state of consciousness also produces its own physiological effects. Cortisol and adrenaline levels decrease. Stress is reduced. Blood pressure goes down. And immune function improves. Brain researchers have shown that when you have the experience of the gap between thoughts, your brain activity is very different from when you are merely awake and alert. This means that glimpsing the soul produces physiological changes, both in the brain and in the body. In this fourth state of consciousness, just as we can glimpse the soul, we can also glimpse the beginnings of synchronicity.

The fifth state of consciousness is called cosmic consciousness. In this state, your spirit can observe your material body. Your awareness goes beyond simply being awake in your body, and beyond simply glimpsing the soul, to being awake and alert to your place as part of the infinite spirit. Even when your body is sleeping, your spirit—the silent observer—is looking at the body in deep sleep, almost as if you were having an out-of-body experience. When that happens there is an alert witnessing awareness, not only when you're sleeping and dreaming, but also when you're fully awake. The spirit is observing, and you are the spirit. The observer can observe the body while it's dreaming, and simultaneously observe the dream. The same experience occurs in wakening consciousness. Your body might be playing a tennis match or speaking on the phone or watching television. All the while, your spirit is observing the body/mind in these activities.

This fifth stage is called cosmic consciousness because you have two qualities to your awareness, local and nonlocal, at the same time. In this fifth state, when you sense your connection to nonlocal intelligence, synchronicity really starts to manifest. In this state, you realize that part of you is localized and part of you, being nonlocal, is connected to everything. You fully live your inseparability to all that exists. Your intuition increases. Your creativity increases. Your insight increases. Research shows that when people have achieved a state of cosmic consciousness such that they have this witnessing experience, their brain waves have the quality of meditation even when they are engaged in activity. These people might be playing soccer, but their brain waves are identical to those of a person who is meditating.

The sixth state of consciousness is called divine consciousness. In this state, the witness becomes more and more awake. In divine consciousness you not only feel the presence of spirit in yourself, but you start to feel that same spirit in all other beings. You see the presence of spirit in plants. Ultimately you feel the presence of spirit in rocks. You recognize that the animating force of life expresses itself in all the objects of the universe, in both the observer and the observed, in both the seer and the scenery. This divine consciousness allows us to see the presence of God in all things. People in a state of divine consciousness are even able to communicate with animals and plants.

This is not a constant state of consciousness for most people. You move in and out of it. But all the great prophets and seers, including Jesus Christ, Buddha, many yogis, and many saints, lived in divine consciousness.

The seventh and last stage of consciousness, the ultimate goal, is called unity consciousness. This may also be called enlightenment. In unity consciousness, the spirit in the perceiver and the spirit in that which is perceived merge and become one.

When this happens, you see the whole world as an extension of your own being. You not only identify with your personal consciousness, but you see that the whole world is a projection of your own self. There's a complete transformation of the personal self into the universal self. In this stage, miracles are commonplace, but they are not even necessary because the infinite realm of possibility is available at every moment. You transcend life. You transcend death. You are the spirit that always was and always will be.

HOW TO MOVE THROUGH THE STAGES OF CONSCIOUSNESS

Synchrodestiny accelerates our ability to advance through the stages of consciousness using four approaches. The first, and most important, is daily meditation. Meditation allows us to glimpse the soul through the gaps between thoughts and discover the silent observer within us. It is the step that allows us to move from the third to the fourth state of consciousness, from being merely awake to being awake and aware of the soul.

The second approach involves practicing recapitulation as described in Chapter 5. Recapitulation allows us to cultivate that silent observer who can move us from the fourth to the fifth state of consciousness. Recapitulation allows us to recognize that what was real during the day is now already part of the dream, just as the reality of a dream fades as we awaken. Just telling yourself, "I'm going to witness my dreams," allows you to experience what people call "lucid dreaming." Soon you can become the choreographer and the director of your dreams, changing them as you go. If you recapitulate your waking day and your dreams, you eventually start to have that experience of witnessing both your dreams and your waking moments.

The third approach involves nurturing relationships, experiencing them as the connection of spirit to spirit, not ego to ego. This facilitates moving to the sixth state of consciousness. Letting go of your need for approval and control accelerates this process. When people are truly in tune with each other, then they experience synchronicity in their relationship. The fourth approach entails reading the sutras. In my experience, if you read the same sentence, the same sutra, every day, that sentence will begin to take on new meanings and engender new experiences as your consciousness or awareness expands. Vedic wisdom holds that "Knowledge is different in different states of consciousness." As your consciousness expands, the same sentences start to take on new nuances of meaning, which in turn yield a deeper understanding. That understanding influences how you experience the world, and those experiences can influence your state of consciousness. With time and practice, you will learn to see the world in ways you never thought possible, full of magic and miracles, fulfilling your heart's every desire.

WHAT TO EXPECT FROM SYNCHRODESTINY

Although the ideas presented in this book can be the beginning of a lifetime of personal evolution and fulfillment, it's up to you to choose whether or not to penetrate the conspiracy of improbabilities and find the hidden treasure that lies behind it. You may start on the path to synchrodestiny as a way to attain wealth, or to find more meaningful relationships, or to become successful in your career. Synchrodestiny certainly can do that for you. But the ultimate goal of synchrodestiny is to expand your consciousness and open a doorway to enlightenment. Enjoy the journey. Each stage brings new wonders, new ways of perceiving and living in the world. Think of synchrodestiny as a kind of rebirth or awakening. Just as your waking days are dramatically different and more exciting than being in a deep sleep, so does awakening to the fifth, sixth, or seventh states of consciousness provide an expansion in what you can experience. Through synchrodestiny, you can finally become the person the universe intended you to be—as powerful as desire, as creative as spirit. All it takes is an eagerness to join the cosmic dance, and a willingness to seek the miracles of the soul.

Once these miracles start to increase as part of your experience of life, you will begin to realize that synchrodestiny is just the symptom of a more profound phenomenon. This profound phenomenon is a shift in your identity and an awakening to who you really are. You begin to understand that the real you is not a person at all. The real you is a field of intelligence in which the person you have identified yourself with, all other persons, as well as the environment in which they exist all co-arise and co-evolve as a result of your own self-interactions. You no longer think of the universe as a sum total of separate and distinct particles but as a coherent, unbroken wholeness in which the personality you currently identify with and its thoughts, all other personalities and their thoughts, and all events and relationships are mutually interdependent, interpenetrating patterns—a single behavior of your nonlocal self. You are the luminous mystery in which the entire universe with all its forms and phenomena arises and subsides. When this realization dawns there is a complete transformation of your personal self into your universal self; there is experiential knowledge of immortality, the complete loss of all fear, including the fear of death. You have become a being that radiates love the same way the sun radiates light. You have finally arrived at the place from which your journey began.

*T*he local self is a transient and impermanent behavior of the nonlocal self. It comes and goes while the nonlocal self continues to evolve into higher experiences of abstraction and creativity.

Don't stand by my grave and weep,
For I am not there.
I do not sleep.
I am a thousand winds that blow,
I am the diamond's glint on snow,
I am the sunlight on ripened grain,
I am the gentle autumn's rain.
In the soft hush of the morning light
I am the swift bird in flight.
Don't stand by my grave and cry,
I am not there,
I did not die.

—UNKNOWN NATIVE AMERICAN AUTHOR

EPILOGUE

In this book you have learned fundamental prac-
tices for achieving the spontaneous fulfillment of
your desires by harnessing the infinite power of
coincidence, or synchronicity. These techniques,
particularly the sutras, are drawn from one of the
world's most ancient wisdom traditions, Vedanta.
In Sanskrit the word *veda* means "knowledge."
Vedanta is the culmination, the peak, or the end
of all knowledge. In other words, Vedanta is the
cream of the Veda.

The core premise of this ancient body of knowledge is that spirit, or consciousness, is the ultimate reality. It is the nonlocal ground of being, which differentiates into objective and subjective reality simultaneously. Subjective reality exists as your thoughts, feelings, emotions, desires, imagination, fantasies, memories, and deepest aspirations. Objective reality is your physical body and the world you experience through your senses. Both these realities coexist simultaneously and interdependently. They do not cause each other, yet they are interdependent. They are *acausally related* to each other. Just as a single cell in the womb differentiates into brain cells, nerve cells, and retinal cells, and through them gives us an experience of the world, so too the single nonlocal spirit becomes both observer and observed, the physical senses and the physical world, the biological organism and its environment, thoughts as well as emotions.

Your inner and outer worlds are both part of a continuum, a single, unified field of activity. The outer world is a mirror of who you are at any particular point in space-time. Many have expressed this idea in various ways. Spiritual teachers tell us if you want to know the state of your personal consciousness, just look around and see what is happening to you. If you want to know the state of the collective consciousness, just look around at what is happening in the world. At any given point in time your personal reality is synchronistically, coincidentally orchestrated by your sense of self.

If your sense of self is constricted, then it expresses itself as a tight and constricted body, a fearful outlook, and an insecure environment. On the other hand, if your sense of self is expanded, it experiences a relaxed body and a friendly, open environment where your intentions synchronistically fulfill themselves. Your expanded self always feels a sense of worth, feels at peace, feels free and unbounded, feels in flow, and feels a sense of awe at the mystery of existence. Sense of self also determines attitude. Greed, arrogance, aggression, and a demanding, disgruntled, and unhappy disposition all arise from a constricted sense of self. Sharing, humility, nurturing, a conciliatory, gracious, and fulfilled disposition all arise from the expanded self.

In the broader sense of self, a critical mass of people in societies, communities, and institutions also determines the attitude of these larger bodies. When a culture has a constricted identity, its emphasis is predominantly on profit-making, ruthless competition, economic imperialism, extreme nationalism, military conflict, violence, and fear. If a critical mass of people were to express their expanded selves, not only would they spontaneously fulfill their personal desires, they would change the very way culture articulates itself. In such a transformed culture the emphasis would be on service rather than on greed, cooperation instead of competition, open hearts instead of only markets. Cultural hallmarks would be nonviolent conflict resolution, compassion, humility, peace, and social and economic justice.

If we look at the world today, we see a tangled hierarchy of interdependently co-arising events. Social scientists claim our collective behavior is creating an unsustainable environment due to depletion of timber, minerals, and fossil fuels, leading to other devastating effects such as the greenhouse effect, changing weather patterns, hurricanes, and rising ocean tides. On the surface these different events don't seem related, but they are. They are the result of our constricted collective sense of self, and they synchronistically, simultaneously co-arise. Religious conflict, pollution, terrorism, depletion of topsoil, nuclear plants, drug addiction, extinction of species, poverty, crime, drug wars, the gun industry, floods and famine, dangerous chemicals in the food chain, and wars are all acausally related.

If each of us could aspire to express the expanded self, and if we could share the knowledge and experience of our expanded selves with one another, perhaps we could create an environment based on respect for life, and achieve a restoration of balance in the oceans, the forests, and the wilderness. This transformed environment would, in turn, result in the simultaneous co-arising of events that would lead to a completely new world. On this ideal planet we would find peace of mind, a sense of the sacred, economic partnerships and prosperity, efficient and clean energy industries, a scientific understanding of the new reality, a flourishing of the arts and philosophy, and a true awareness of our inseparability. In such a society we would see clearly that love is the ultimate force at the heart of the universe.

*Y*our ability to spontaneously fulfill your desires is directly proportional to your experience of your nonlocal self. Although the wisdom traditions, particularly Vedanta, give us deep insight into the nature of nonlocal reality, only recently have scientists begun to explore this domain of existence. Throughout this book I have emphasized this new, scientific basis for the understanding of synchronicity and the spontaneous fulfillment of desire. The Chopra Foundation is actively involved in collaborative studies with scientists to further explore the scientific basis of nonlocality.

The following is a subjective, selected list of references for further reading on nonlocality. Some of the entries, including certain scientific journals, are quite technical, and may not be easy to understand without a scientific background. Other sources, such as Larry Dossey's book

Healing Words, are very accessible. In either event this list is offered in the hope that you will use it to deepen your understanding of the world where we are all instantly connected, where we are, in fact, inseparably one.

SELECTED
REFERENCES ON
NONLOCALITY

Astin, J. A., Harkness, E., and Ernst, E. (2000). "The efficacy of 'distant healing': a systematic review of randomized trials." *Ann Intern Med* *132*(11), 903–910.

Bastyr University of Washington and the Chopra Center on Neural Energy Transfers Between Individuals Who Have Undergone Chopra Center for Well-Being Programs. A joint collaboration. *Private communication.*

Braud, W. G. (1990). "Distant mental influence on rate of hemolysis of human red blood cells." *J Am Soc Psychical Res 84,* 1–24.

Braud W., Shafer, D., and Andrews, S. (1993). "Further studies of autonomic detection of remote starring: replications, new control procedures, and personality correlates." *J Parapsychol 57,* 391–409.

Byrd, R. C. (1988). "Positive therapeutic effects of intercessory prayer in a coronary care unit population." *Southern Med J 81*(7), 826–829.

Delanoy, D. L., and Sah, S. (1994). "Cognitive and physiological psi responses to remote positive and neutral states." From proceedings of presented papers, 37th Annual Parapsychological Association Convention, Amsterdam, The Netherlands, 128–138.

Dossey, L. (1993). *Healing Words: The Power of Prayer and the Practice of Medicine.* San Francisco: HarperCollins.

Grinberg-Zylberbaum, J., Delaflor, M., Attie, L., and Goswami, A. (1994). "The Einstein-Podolsky-Rosen Paradox in the Brain: The Transferred Potential" (physics essays). *Rare manuscripts.*

Harris, W. S., Gowda, M., Kolb, J. W., Strachacz, C. P., Vacek, J. L., Jones, P. G., Forker, A.,

O'Keefe, J. H., and McCallister, B. D. (1999). "A randomized, controlled trial of the effects of remote intercessory prayer on outcomes in patients admitted to the coronary care unit."

Krucoff, M. W. (2000). "Growing the path to the patient: an editorial outlook for alternative therapies." *Altern Ther Health Med* 6(4), 36–37.

Krucoff, M., et al. (2001). "Integrative noetic therapies as adjuncts to percutaneous intervention during unstable coronary syndromes: monitoring and actualization of noetic training (MANTRA) feasibility pilot." *American Heart Journal* 142(5), 760–767.

Kwang, Y., et al. (2001). "Does prayer influence the success of in vitro fertilization–embryo transfer?" *J Repro Med* 46(9), 1–8.

Nash, C. B. (1982). "Psychokinetic control of bacterial growth." *J Am Soc Psychical Res* 51, 217–221.

Radin, D. I. (1997). *The Conscious Universe: The Scientific Truth of Psychic Phenomena*. New York: HarperEdge.

Schlitz, M. J. (1995). "Intentionality in healing: mapping the integration of body, mind, and spirit." *Alternative Therapies* 1(5), 119–120.

————. (1996). "Intentionality and intuition and their clinical implications: a challenge for science and medicine." *Advances* 12(2), 58–66.

Schlitz, M., and Braud, W. (1991). "Consciousness interactions with remote biological systems: anomalous intentionality effects." *Subtle Energies* 1, 1–20.

————. (1997). "Distant intentionality and healing: assessing the evidence." *Alternative Therapies* 3(6), 62–73.

Schlitz, M., and Harman, W. (1999). "The implications of alternative and complementary medicine for science and the scientific process." In *Essentials of Complementary and Alternative Medicine.* Edited by W. B. Jonas and J. S. Levin. Philadelphia: Williams & Wilkins.

Schlitz, M., and LaBerge, S. (1994). "Autonomic detection of remote observation: two conceptual replications." From proceedings of presented papers, 37th Annual Parapsychological Association Convention, Amsterdam, The Netherlands, 352–364.

Schlitz, M., and Lewis, N. (1996, Summer). "The healing powers of prayer." *Noetic Sciences Review,* 29–33.

Schlitz, M., Taylor, E., and Lewis, N. (1998, Winter). "Toward a noetic model of medicine." *Noetic Sciences Review*, 45–52.

Schwartz, G., and Chopra, D. "Nonlocal anomalous information retrieval: a multi-medium multi-scored single-blind experiment." *Private communication.*

Snel, F. W., and van der Sijde, P. C. (1994). "Information-processing styles of paranormal healers." *Psychol Rep* 74(2), 363–366.

Stapp, H. P. (1994). "Theoretical model of a purported empirical violation of the predictions of quantum theory." *Am Physical Soc* 50(1): 18–22.

Targ, E. (1997). "Evaluating distant healing: a research review." *Altern Ther Health Med* 3(6), 74–78.

————. (2002). "Research methodology for studies of prayer and distant healing." *Complement Ther Nurs Midwifery* 8(1), 29–41.

Wilber K. (1996). *A Brief History of Everything.* Boston: Shambhala.

Wirth, D. P. (1995). "Complementary healing intervention and dermal wound reepithelialization: an overview." *Int J Psychosom* 42(1–4), 48–53.

*T*he Chopra Foundation, a nonprofit institution, has partnered with leaders throughout the world to create an "alliance for the new humanity," based on the principles you have learned in this book. This alliance includes Nobel laureates, economists, and other luminaries, and has as its goal "the awakening of the neural networks of the planetary mind to create a critical mass of peace consciousness." Peace consciousness is not antiwar activism but the basis for manifesting the world we all want for ourselves and for future generations. If you would like to join existing "peace cells," or to create peace cells of your own, please go to our website, www.chopra.com, and through it visit the website for the alliance. We sincerely hope you'll join us.

Understanding the nature of the nonlocal self is such an important yet elusive task that I have included the following appendices for those readers interested in exploring this fascinating subject further. The first appendix articulates much of what we have already learned, but this time we shift from a historical and philosophical perspective with roots in the ancient East to the great early civilizations of Greece, Rome, and Egypt. As always, there is value to be derived from seeing things from a fresh point of view. The second appendix uses a story from one of the great Vedic texts to illustrate "that which cannot be seen but makes seeing possible, that which cannot be known but makes knowing possible, that which cannot be imagined but makes imagination possible."

I hope you will find these additions helpful.

—D.C.

APPENDIX A

In the previous pages we have explored how the nonlocal self differentiates into the cosmos, and we have also learned how to make practical use of this knowledge for the spontaneous fulfillment of desire. To these ends the wisdom tradition of Vedanta has been reinterpreted in our modern, contemporary, scientific framework. Lest you, the reader, think that this knowledge exists only in the esoteric schools of the East, I offer in the following paragraphs closely parallel insights from hermetic philosophy, or hermeticism as it is also known, which have been passed down to us through the ages from ancient schools in Greece, Rome, and Egypt.

Hermeticism is a mystical philosophy that deals with magic, alchemy, and other manifestations from the spiritual into the material world. The origin of hermetic knowledge traces back to Hermes Trismagistus, about whom not much is known, including the date or place of his birth. Scholars suppose that he lived around 2,000 B.C.E. Many think he was an Egyptian priest, the inventor of both art and science as we know them in the western world. The mystery of Hermes Magistus—"the three-time great"—was addressed by both Greek and Roman mystics in various ancient documents. Mythology has elevated him to the rank of a god, perhaps the ibis-headed moon god Thoth, the Egyptian god of healing, intelligence, and letters. According to one tradition, Thoth was the architect of the great pyramids of Giza.

Over the last two millennia hermetic wisdom has been a source for a variety of Gnostic writings or teachings. It is not clear whether these were originally the teachings of one person or in fact the mystical visions of several seers of Greek, Roman, and Egyptian origin. In any event the fundamental tenets of hermetic philosophy can be summarized in the following insights or principles.

*   *   *

The first insight is that everything is a manifestation of spirit. Spirit is the state of being that gives rise to space, time, causation, matter, and energy. Infinite and unbounded, spirit contains the entire universe that we experience. Nothing exists outside it. Spirit is the source of the whole chain of being, the whole of existence. The universe arises from spirit, is contained in it and ultimately disappears back into it. This is the first insight, which provides us with a very clear description of the nonlocal domain.

The second insight is that as spirit becomes manifest, it does so in such a way that the whole is contained in every part. Today's science calls this the holographic model—that the whole is contained in every part. As atoms reflect the universe, so too does the human body reflect the cosmic body and the human mind the cosmic mind. What does this mean? It proposes that in any one thing you behold, indeed in every conceivable thing you can imagine, there also exists the latent potentiality for all things—for absolutely everything. The whole universe is contained in every point just as the whole ocean is reflected in every drop within its depths. In Vedanta this insight is expressed as "What is here is everywhere, and what is not here is nowhere."

This principle means that you don't have to go

in search of anything to find the truth. The truth is always right here, staring at you in the face. So when we wonder, "If there are human beings here, does that mean that life exists elsewhere in the universe?" the answer is absolutely yes. Exploring the molecule is like exploring the galaxy. Similarly, everything is contained in the ground of your own being. Rumi says the whole universe is contained within your self, and this is a fundamental truth. According to biblical literature the kingdom of Heaven is within you. The treasure house lies right here, before you. In the New Testament Jesus says, "Ask and you shall receive. Knock and it shall be opened unto you. Seek and you will find."

Our educational system is based on accumulating more and more information, but actually the more information we gather, the more confused we become and the more we lose sight of the wisdom that is already inherent within us. So learn to ask the truth of yourself. Learn to knock on the door of your own being. This is what is known as intuition, creativity, vision, and prophecy. This is why a sage is focused on the seer and not the scenery. The seer is the nonlocal self.

The third insight states that everything is vibration, that consciousness consists of vibrations in various frequencies, resulting in all the forms and phenomena of the universe. Human beings are conscious energy fields, along with the rest of the universe. If you want to change the world around you, you need only change the quality of your own vibration; as you change that, the quality of what is around you changes. Incidentally, this is the reason why sutras work. They provide one particular way to create a certain vibration of spirit, or a particular flavor of the nonlocal self.

The situations, circumstances, events, and relationships that you encounter in your life are a reflection of the state of consciousness you are in. The world is a mirror. If you are anchored in your nonlocal self the whole world is available to you.

*T*he fourth insight is that change is the only constant. Everything is impermanent. Holding on to anything is like holding on to your breath; if you hold on long enough, you'll suffocate. Ultimately the only way to acquire anything in the physical universe is to let go of it and not hold on.

This is a very delicate point. It means that the best results are achieved when we focus on process rather than on outcome. Focusing on the outcome creates anxiety and stress, which interferes with the spontaneous flow of intelligence as it moves from the unmanifest domain (spirit) to the manifest domain (the material world). The fact that change is the only constant means that we are always living in the unknown.

Everything that we call the known is past, and

the only thing we can say about it with certainty is that it is no longer here. The known is the prison of past conditioning. The unknown is always fresh, which is a quality of the field of infinite possibilities. Zen masters, martial artists, and great spiritual teachers have always advised that we must go with the flow. The flow is the field of change. What doesn't change decays and dies. Change is the dance and rhythm of the universe. To have one-pointed intention, to flow with the change, and to be detached from outcome at the same time: These are the mechanics of the fulfillment of desire, which orchestrates synchrodestiny.

*T*he fifth insight is that everything, whether it is an experience or an attitude or an object, contains its opposite. In fact, whatever you have right now, good or bad, contains its counterpart. No matter how deep you may be in the depths of depression, for example, if you identify its opposite—joy or gratitude—and pay attention to it, you'll see that it starts to grow in your awareness. Removing your attention from despair and placing it on happiness actually makes the new feeling blossom. Similarly, if you're at the heights of ecstasy, be aware that its opposite walks by its side. By being mindful of this principle—that all of creation is based on the co-creation and co-existence of opposites—you can use the quality of your attention to bring out whatever aspect of experience you desire.

*   *   *

*T*he sixth insight states that there is a rhythm to everything. The life cycle provides a classic example: Conception is followed by gestation, birth, growth, maturity, death, and renewal. All things happen in cycles. Synchronicity involves appreciating that the cycles and seasons of life are coordinated with the cycles and seasons of the cosmos. According to a Chinese expression, "Spring flowers, summer breeze, autumn leaves, and winter snow: If you are totally tuned in, this is the best season of your life." When you are grounded in life-centered, present-moment awareness, you are in touch with your nonlocal self, which orchestrates the dance of the universe. When your rhythms are in harmony with the rhythms of the universe, synchrodestiny works its magic.

*T*he seventh insight states that every event has infinite causes that lead to an infinity of effects. The so-called "cause/effect relationship" is not linear. We have explored this principle as "interdependent co-arising," the phenomenon that allows us to use synchrodestiny to see the patterns behind every event.

*T*he eighth insight posits that the creative energy of the universe is also reflected as sexual energy. All things that exist are born from this primal energy. A child is born out of it. A flower blossoms through that energy, as does a fruit. Nothing in creation is exempt from this principle. In human beings this primal energy manifests as passion, excitement, and arousal. When we are in touch with our nonlocal self we spontaneously experience enthusiasm and inspiration. The word *enthusiasm* contains two roots: "en" and "theos." This means to be one with God, or the nonlocal self. (The word *inspiration* similarly means "to be one with spirit.") Inspiration, enthusiasm, passion, and excitement give energy to our intentions and thus accelerate the spontaneous fulfillment of our desires.

The ninth insight says that we can direct primal energy through the power of attention and intention. As we've seen, whatever we put our attention on (and thereby make the focus of this energy) blossoms. Whatever we withdraw our attention from starts to wither away. Attention and intention are the keys to transformation, whether it is of a situation, circumstance, person, or thing. The sutras in this book are codes for triggering and activating intention and attention.

The tenth insight states that we can achieve harmony through those forces and elements in the cosmos that we call masculine and feminine. A hermetic philosophy called "the principles of gender" proposes that true passion can only occur if there's a balance between the masculine and feminine forces in your own being. Masculine energy drives qualities such as aggression, decisiveness, action, and courage, whereas feminine energy can be seen in an appreciation for beauty, intuition, nurturing, affection, and tenderness. Great works of art always contain the harmonious interaction of masculine and feminine, yin and yang. The sutra *shiva shakti* is meant to activate the harmonious interaction of the masculine and feminine archetypal energies of your nonlocal self.

The eleventh insight posits that the inner nature of every being, no matter how evil it may seem to be, is love, and that this essential quality can always be revealed by unmasking our own love. Love, therefore, is not a mere sentiment; it is the ultimate truth at the heart of all creation. It is unconditional and unbounded, and it radiates from us when we are in touch with our nonlocal self.

These eleven principles then are the principles of alchemy found in the work of Hermes Trismagistus, Vedanta, and indeed in all the perennial philosophies of humanity. Once we have absorbed these insights, then our own inner attitudes, our thoughts, our dreams, and our feelings in response to various situations become much more expansive. For example, by becoming fully attuned to the cycles, the rhythms, and the seasons of life, we never get distressed or overshadowed by one particular situation.

The following story, which derives from one of the greatest Vedantic texts, the Chandogya Upanishad, beautifully describes the nature of the nonlocal self.

Thousands of years ago the great sage Uddalaka Aruni sent his twelve-year-old son, Svetaketu, to a great guru so that the boy could learn deeply about the ultimate reality. For a dozen years Svetaketu studied under his master and memorized all the Vedas. When Svetaketu returned home, his father noticed that his son acted as though he had learned all there was to learn. So Uddalaka decided to pose the young man a question.

"My learned son, what is that thing which cannot be heard but makes hearing possible, which cannot be seen but makes seeing possible, which cannot be known but makes knowledge possible, which cannot be imagined but makes imagination possible?"

Svetaketu was perplexed and silent.

His father said, "When we know a single particle of clay, all objects of clay are known. When we know a single grain of gold, all objects of gold are known. The difference between one piece of golden jewelry and another is only in its name and form. In reality all the jewelry is just gold, and all the pots are just clay. Can you tell me, my son, what is that one thing which by knowing all can be known?"

Svetaketu replied, "Alas, my master did not give me this knowledge. Will you?"

"Very well," said Uddalaka. "Let me tell you.

"The whole universe is one reality, and that reality is pure consciousness. Pure consciousness is absolute existence. It is One that is not followed by a Second. In the beginning the One said to itself, 'I shall differentiate into the many, and so become all the seers and all the scenery.' The One entered into the many, and became the Self of each. The beings of all things are the One, and that One is the subtle essence of all that exists. You are that, Svetaketu.

"In this same way bees make honey from the nectar of numerous flowers, but once the honey is made the nectar cannot say, 'I am from this flower, or that.' So too, when you merge with your non-local Self you become one with the Self of all that exists. This is the true Self of all, and Svetaketu, you are that."

The young man replied, "Enlighten me more, my father."

Uddalaka paused before speaking. "The river Ganges flows to the east. The river Indus flows to the west. However, they both ultimately become the sea. Having become the sea they no longer think 'I am the Ganges' or 'I am the Indus.' So too, my son, everything that exists has its source in the nonlocal Self, and that Self is the subtlest essence of all. It is the true Self. Svetaketu, you are that.

"When the body withers and dies, the Self does not die. Fire cannot burn it, water cannot wet it, wind cannot dry it, weapons cannot shatter it. It is unborn, has no beginning or ending. It is beyond the boundaries of space and time, pervading the entire universe. Svetaketu, you are that."

"Enlighten me more, father," Svetaketu responded enthusiastically.

Uddelaka said, "Bring me a fruit of the *nya-grodha* tree."

Svetaketu brought the fruit.

"Break it open."

Svetaketu did so.

"What do you see, my son?"

"Tiny seeds, father."

"Break one now."

Svetaketu broke open the tiny seed.

"What do you see, my son?"

"I see that nothing is left, father."

"That which you do not see is the subtle essence, and the whole of the *nyagrodha* tree comes from it. So too the universe sprouts forth from the nonlocal Self."

Finally Uddelaka asks Svetaketu to place a cube of salt into a pail of water. The next day the sage asked his son to give him back the cube of salt.

"I cannot give it back," the young man responded. "It has dissolved."

Uddelaka asked his son to taste the surface of the water. "Tell me, how is it?"

"It is salty, father."

"Taste it in the middle, and see how it is."

"It is salty, father."

"Taste it at the bottom, and tell me how it is."

"It is salty, father."

"Just like the salt is localized in the cube and dispersed in the water, so too your Self is simultaneously localized in your body and pervading the entire universe.

"My dear son," Uddelaka said. "You do not perceive the Self in your body, but without it perceptions would not be possible. You cannot conceptualize the Self, but without it conceptualization would not be possible. You cannot imagine the Self, but without it imagination would not be possible. However, when you become the Self and live from the level of this nonlocal Self, you will be connected to all that exists, because the Self is the source of all that exists. Truth, reality, existence, consciousness, the absolute—call it what you will, it is the ultimate reality, the ground of all being. And you are that, Svetaketu.

"Live from this level, Svetaketu, and all your desires will come true because from this level they will not just be your personal desires, they will be aligned with the desires of all that exists."

Svetaketu practiced all that he had learned and became one of the greatest seers of the Vedantic tradition.

INDEX

ABOUT THE AUTHOR

Deepak Chopra's books have become international bestsellers and classics of their kind. Dr. Chopra is founder of the Chopra Center for Well Being in Carlsbad, California. Visit his website at www.chopra.com.

Deepak Chopra and The Chopra Center for Well Being at La Costa Resort and Spa, Carlsbad, California, offer a wide range of seminars, products and educational programmes, worldwide. The Chopra Center offers revitalizing mind/body programmes, as well as day spa services. Guests can come to rejuvenate, expand knowledge or obtain a medical consultation.

For information on meditation classes, health and well-being courses, instructor certification programmes, or local classes in your area, contact The Chopra Center for Well Being at La Costa Resort and Spa, 7321 Estrella Del Mar Road, Carlsbad, CA 92009-6725, USA. By telephone: 001-888-424-6772, or 001-760-931-7509. For a virtual tour of the Center, visit the Internet website at www.chopra.com.

If you live in Europe and would like more information on workshops, lectures or other programmes about Dr. Deepak Chopra or to order any of his books, tapes or products, please contact: Contours, 44 Fordbridge Road, Ashford, Middlesex, TW15 2SJ (tel: +44 (0) 208 564 7033; fax (0) 208 897 3807; email: sales@infinite-contours.co.uk; website: www.infinite-contours.co.uk).

If you live in Australia and would like more information on workshops, lextures, or programmes presented by Dr. Deepak Chopra, please contact What's On The Planet Pty Ltd, PO Box 161, Brighton Le Sands, NSW 2216, Australia, or email deepak@theplanet.com.au.

Rider books are available from all good bookshops or by ordering direct on 01624 677237. Or visit our website at www.randomhouse.co.uk.